Advance Praise for
Sales Management. Simplified.

"If you want a clear and concise overview of exactly what you need to do to run a superstar sales team, this is the book for you. Mike takes his years of experience and shares with you his best ideas on how to make successful sales management...simple. I highly recommend this book to anyone in sales."

—**John Spence, author of** *Awesomely Simple*

"Weinberg has clearly and simply laid out the recipe for success in sales management in this easy-to-read and easy-to-follow common sense book. I will be distributing it to all my fellow business owners and clients as mandatory reading for growth and profit improvement."

—**Gina Hoagland, President, Collaborative Strategies, Inc.**

"This is the first blunt, spot-on sales management book that will unsettle you to the core about how you lead people. A must-read for every sales manager, for every salesperson to buy for their manager, and for anyone who wants to be a manager!"

—**Mark Hunter, "The Sales Hunter," and author of** *High-Profit Selling*

"Weinberg's book drips with the common sense wisdom of experience. Topic after topic, he finds the sweet spot between sound theory and practical advice. The chapters on manager conversations and business plans are worth the price alone! Stock up on highlighter pens – you'll need them."

—**Charles Green, CEO, Trusted Advisor Associates,
and co-author of** *The Trusted Advisor*

"Wow! This is the best book for sales leaders I have read in 20 years. If you're not afraid of the truth and serious about getting better, use this guide to transform your sales team. Merci, Mike!"

—**Sebastien Zuchowski, Vice President, Marketing & Sales, ERP Guru**

"Mike's book does exactly what it needs to for executives: Part One unsettles you by holding a mirror uncomfortably close while Part Two delivers a SIMPLE, straightforward plan to improve your sales team."

—**Bill Hinderer, President, Tacony Corporation**

"I have always believed you can't learn Sales Management from a book; you just have to get engaged and learn along the way. *Sales Management. Simplified.* has caused me to revise my thinking. You still need to get engaged, but you can't have a better reference to accelerate your learning than Mike's book."

—Dave Brock, CEO, Partners in EXCELLENCE

"Reading this book is like having a direct, no-nonsense conversation with Mike. He delivers fantastic advice and insights, and fills his chapt ers with takeaways that will benefit sales managers of all experience levels. I even found great strategies to use when 'managing' my sales students! *New Sales. Simplified.* is required reading for my Advanced Selling class, and I guarantee that *Sales Management. Simplified.* will play a key role in the Sales Force Leadership class I teach."

—Dawn Deeter, Ph.D., Professor & Chair of Relational Selling and Marketing; Director, Kansas State University National Strategic Selling Institute

"*Sales Management. Simplified.* is the real deal for executives and sales managers. We know first hand from working with Mike that these principles work!"

—Jeff Haller, Founder and CEO, DataServ

"Mike uses real-world practical examples of effective sales management and leadership principles seasoned with a good dose of humor to keep the reader engaged. Reading this book is a must for every sales leader who is serious about improving sales team performance!"

—Brian Layman, Vice President, Business Development, Mack Trucks

"Mike Weinberg's *Sales Management. Simplified.* is going to start a sales management revolution. Every chapter I couldn't help but say yes! yes! and yes! I am going to recommend that all my clients get a copy and so should you!"

—Steven A. Rosen, Founder of Star Results and author of *52 Sales Management Tips3*

SALES MANAGEMENT.

SIMPLIFIED.

THE STRAIGHT TRUTH ABOUT GETTING EXCEPTIONAL RESULTS FROM YOUR SALES TEAM

MIKE WEINBERG

AMACOM

AMERICAN MANAGEMENT ASSOCIATION

New York · Atlanta · Brussels · Chicago · Mexico City · San Francisco
Shanghai · Tokyo · Toronto · Washington, D.C.

This publication is designed to provide accurate and authoritative information in regard to the subject matter covered. It is sold with the understanding that the publisher is not engaged in rendering legal, accounting, or other professional service. If legal advice or other expert assistance is required, the services of a competent professional person should be sought.

LIBRARY OF CONGRESS CATALOGING-IN-PUBLICATION DATA
Weinberg, Mike, 1967-
  Sales management : simplified : the straight truth about getting exceptional results from your sales team / Mike Weinberg. — First Edition.
      pages cm
  Includes bibliographical references and index.
  ISBN 978-0-8144-3643-1 (hardcover) — ISBN 978-0-8144-3644-8 (ebook)
  1. Selling. 2. Business planning. I. Title.
  HF5438.25.W29295 2015
  658.8'1—dc23
2015015644

About AMA
American Management Association (www.amanet.org) is a world leader in talent development, advancing the skills of individuals to drive business success. Our mission is to support the goals of individuals and organizations through a complete range of products and services, including classroom and virtual seminars, webcasts, webinars, podcasts, conferences, corporate and government solutions, business books, and research. AMA's approach to improving performance combines experiential learning—learning through doing—with opportunities for ongoing professional growth at every step of one's career journey.

Printing number

10 9 8 7 6 5 4 3

For Corey, Haley, and Kurt.
I love you and am more proud
of you than I can possibly express.

CONTENTS

PART ONE

Blunt Truth from the Front Lines:
Why So Many Sales Organizations Fail to Produce the Desired Results

CONTENTS

PART TWO

Practical Help and a Simple Framework
to Get Exceptional Results from Your Sales Team

FOREWORD

In a recent LinkedIn Pulse article, a CEO in the tech industry declared that he would never again hire salespeople. The post went viral to cheers and jeers, and was viewed and shared hundreds of thousands of times on LinkedIn.

While the premise of the article was absurd, it clearly struck a nerve and brought to the surface highly charged emotions, including a deep animosity toward sales in general. It also revealed how desperate businesses are for a solution to the #1 problem plaguing twenty-first century companies: underperforming salespeople in dysfunctional and sub-optimized sales organizations.

Sadly, many of the problems that front-line sales management and senior executives face with their sales organizations are self-inflicted. In *Sales Management. Simplified.*, Mike Weinberg does a brilliant job of laying this truth bare. And while doing so, he delivers an unequaled blueprint for both leading salespeople and building high-performance sales teams.

This is arguably the best book that has ever been written on sales management, and I don't say this lightly. I've read virtually every book on the subject published over the last 20 years and have dedicated my career to building better sales leaders. When it comes to sales leadership, I know awesome when I see it.

With real-life examples, authenticity, honesty, and common sense, Mike conquers the three core pillars of sales leadership—*leading, managing,* and *coaching*—and provides you with the concepts and tools you'll need to be effective and proficient in each.

The first half of the book is loud—so loud it will shake you out of your comfort zone as it delivers a blunt wake-up call that clearly illustrates why your sales team isn't delivering results. You'll come face to face with the destructive leadership attitudes and behaviors that are holding your sales organization back. The second half of the book then offers a simple model for sales leadership as well as practical advice on the essentials of sales management that you can begin using immediately.

Here's the brutal truth, though, that you must embrace. Regardless of your organizational role, as a leader, if your sales team succeeds, you succeed. If your team fails, you fail, your company fails, and all of the employees that work for your company fail. Without sales, without customers, you have no company. Period. End of story. Sales leadership is that important.

Sales Management. Simplified. gets you upfront and personal with the undeniable fact that your job as a leader is to create a healthy, results-focused culture where your salespeople can develop their skills, leverage their talents, and thrive. Mike reminds you that to drive long-term success, you must *"make heroes, not be the hero."* All roadblocks, including your own ego-driven interference, must be relentlessly removed in order for your team to deliver on the number that everyone in your organization counts on for survival.

This might be a good time to pause and strap yourself in. You're about to go on a high-octane journey to higher sales productivity. I promise that it's going to be one heck of a ride.

Jeb Blount, CEO of Sales Gravy & author of
People Follow You: The Real Secret to What Matters Most in Leadership

ACKNOWLEDGMENTS

Big-time thanks and props to my editor at AMACOM, Bob Nirkind, for pushing me to do this book and for being an invaluable resource from beginning to end. He has become a good friend, and I wish him a most wonderful retirement. And a special nod to Michael Sivilli for all his help, and for shepherding the project to conclusion.

To Edward Davidheiser, my step grandfather, mentor, consultant, and friend, who passed on during the writing of this book; and to the classy Lois Davidheiser, for her strength, wise perspective, and encouragement. To my dad, for sharing mountains of sales wisdom over the years, and to my mom and stepmom for their constant cheerleading and inflated view of me, I thank them!

To my incredible team: Mary Oliver and Bryan Miles of eaHelp, and to Krissy McArthur and Miles Austin, huge appreciation for everything they do, for making me look good, and for keeping my head from exploding. And to Shane Johnston, Rob Morton, and Mark Peterman, my wise friends and trusted advisors for whom I could not be more appreciative; and to my friend and former business partner, Donnie Williams, who modeled and taught sales leadership with the very best of them.

To the world's greatest kids, Corey, Haley, and Kurt, my pride and joy, thanks for their support, love, and inspiration. And the biggest thank you of all goes to Katie, my bride and best friend, for her encouragement, brains, and editing, and for finding a way for me to write this book in the midst of our crazy-busy life, two college searches, and our day jobs.

INTRODUCTION

I love sales and helping salespeople excel at developing new business. But what I love even more is experiencing a high-performance, results-focused, winning sales team with solid leadership, smart talent management, a strong sales culture, and a sound sales process. My two primary goals in writing *Sales Management. Simplified.* are to bluntly share the reasons so few sales organizations today exhibit these characteristics, and to offer a simple, actionable framework that sales managers and senior executives can adopt to create dramatic and lasting sales performance improvement.

I was compelled to write this book because of what I'm observing in companies where I consult, coach, and speak. Everywhere I turn, sales managers are overwhelmed and often confused, and executives are frustrated. Managers are working harder and longer than ever, yet accomplishing less. The *noise* from supposed sales "experts" is deafening. We have more sales tools, toys, gimmicks, and processes than any human being could possibly digest, and we are constantly being told that "everything has changed." Instead of returning to the tried-and-true basics of sales management, sales leaders live daily searching for new answers.

This book is divided into two distinct parts. Part One delivers the straight truth about why so many sales organizations are failing to deliver the desired results. Be forewarned: I did not hold back or mince words. My intention is for Chapters 1–16 to serve as a loud wakeup call. Very often, what is believed to be a sales problem turns out to be a leadership and culture problem. So, if you are a sales leader or a corporate executive and your salespeople gave you this book, please don't hold it against them. Be angry with me for stirring the pot. If they had the guts to ask you to read this, believe me, they want to succeed as badly as you do!

In Part One you will read true stories about real sales managers and real executives in real companies, big and small. My hope is that seeing their situations will cause you to pause and take a long look in the mirror to evaluate yours with fresh eyes and a new perspective.

I'll tackle topics ranging from company leadership diverting and distracting sales managers from their primary job and burying them with unimaginable amounts of crap, to silly compensation plans that reward salespeople for babysitting customers acquired years ago. I shine the spotlight on self-proclaimed "sales expert" executives who deflate salespeople with their pontificating and micromanagement, while also reminding charismatic, visionary entrepreneurs that their salespeople require a tad more clarity and support than they tend to realize.

After reading Part One, sales managers may think twice before putting on the fire chief's helmet and attempting to solve their company's every problem. Hopefully, many will come to agree that you can't effectively lead a sales team via email or with your head buried in CRM screens! And above all, sales managers will become convinced that much of their time is spent on low-value, low-payoff activities instead of on the sales leadership essentials outlined in the second half of the book.

Part Two presents a very simple, practical sales management framework that any company or leader can implement. We will examine the characteristics of a healthy sales culture and learn how to create one. Managers will be challenged to radically reorient their calendars to maximize time spent on high-value activities that include conducting regular results-focused 1:1 meetings with each of their people; leading productive sales team meetings that energize, equip, and align their teams; and working alongside salespeople as a true coach, manager, and mentor.

In Chapter 18, I take you behind the scenes for an in-depth look at the single healthiest sales culture I've ever experienced. Chapter 20 offers practical tips to significantly ramp up accountability without coming across as a micromanager or demotivating salespeople. Chapter 21 not only paints the picture of what sales team meetings can be, but also offers ideas for agenda items and help for exhausted sales managers who carry too much of the burden for leading sales meetings.

Chapter 23 challenges you to rethink the sales roles at your company as I make my best case that zookeepers won't hunt no matter how hard you push them—and that you'd have more sales if your few true hunters were freed up to do more of what they do best. I also describe practical ways to keep your A-players happy and on your team, and how to coach up or coach out your underperformers quickly.

Chapters 24 through 26 cover the sales leader's responsibilities to point the team toward strategic targets, to arm the team with the weapons necessary to win, and to monitor the battle in real time. These managers also get one final reminder that they're ultimately judged by the results of their team, not the amount of *work* they do. Therefore, they must master the art of becoming *selfishly productive* to take back control of their calendars and focus on the sales management essentials that truly move the performance needle.

Thank you for joining me on this journey to first look at what may be hindering sales performance and then at simple ways you can start getting exceptional results from your sales team.

PART ONE

Blunt Truth from the Front Lines

Why So Many Sales Organizations Fail to Produce the Desired Results

CHAPTER 1

As Goes the Leader, So Goes the Organization

I can point to the exact spot on the Highway 40 exit to Ballas Road where I finally gave in and called my dad. After an incredible ten-plus-year run as a top-producing salesperson for various companies and another successful, fun four years coaching salespeople and sales teams how to develop new business, I was struggling mightily in my first sales management role.

For the life of me, I couldn't figure it out. How could I be struggling so badly after so many years as both a top individual producer and a highly respected sales coach? So, what does a thirty-eight-year-old clueless executive do when he's out of ideas and tired of banging his head against the wall? Darn right. He picks up the phone to call his dad. Not just any dad, but the former big-time New York City sales executive dad who'd forgotten more about sales management than I ever hoped to know.

The Real Life of the Sales Leader

My dad answered the phone, and I exploded, cathartically blasting him with a litany of challenges weighing on me. If only I'd had the presence of mind to record that phone call, which went something like this:

"I've never worked longer or harder yet spent so little time on what moves the needle. I have zero control of my days. My weak salespeople are afraid of their own shadow and need constant baby-sitting; the strong ones are high-maintenance and nothing is ever good enough for them. The CEO thinks he's a sales expert, but con-tinually deflates the sales team with his overbearing pontificating about various topics. The CFO sends me spreadsheets in a six-point font with embedded pivot tables to demonstrate how we're over-discounting. I don't even know what a pivot table is, let alone how to use one! The manufacturers we represent continually pester me looking to schedule time in the field with my people. I feel like a logistics manager, not a sales leader! The internal marketing people are ticked that we're behind placing a new line of displays. Our big competitor just stole our number one guy because our compensation plan is too flat. Other department heads keep inviting me to meet-ings that have nothing to do with generating revenue. And some idiot customer service rep is giving out my cell phone number to customers with technical questions that I can't answer. That's how I'm doing, Dad. Glad you asked?"

My dad waited about five seconds, which felt like an eternity, before responding, and then he said one word: "Congratulations."

I was none too pleased with his sarcasm. Huh? Come again, big fella? Then he continued:

"Congratulations, Michael. You now understand that the front-line sales management role is one of the absolute toughest jobs on the planet. Everyone wants a piece of you, just like you described. There's no way to win without a solid grounding in your absolute priorities and a laser focus on what's absolutely critical to drive the business. None of those people placing demands on you and putting work on your desk understands your job. And if you let them dictate how to spend your time, you'll not only be miserable like you are now, but you'll also fail."

Wiser words have never been spoken. And so began my next ten-year journey—a mission to master sales management and help others do the same.

You Don't Transform Organizations from the Bottom

Along with my painful yet formative first go-round as a sales executive there was another strong motivator pushing me to unlock the keys to successful sales leadership. During my initial stint in consulting and coaching, I learned the hard way that while I could improve the performance of individual producers by teaching and coaching my New Sales Driver framework (highlighted in my first book, *New Sales. Simplified.* [New York: AMACOM, 2013]), that was not enough to transform sales organizations. Organizations don't change from the bottom by improving the skills, techniques, and attitudes of their salespeople. To truly transform the results and health of an entire sales team, the leader and the culture must be transformed.

As you'll read in many of the true stories and anecdotes I share in Part One of this book, the sales *problem* in many businesses I consult with does not lie with the salespeople. The main challenge is typically how the sales team is being led, and more often than not, the underlying root cause issues are cultural, flowing down from leadership at the top of the company.

That same CEO I mentioned in my call to my dad, the one who liked to pontificate about sales, also happened to be a brilliant, well-read consultant who had worked with dozens and dozens of business owners, senior executives, and organizations. When it came to leadership and organizational behavior, he was a hugely valuable mentor to me and probably had the sharpest business mind I'd encountered. He taught me a ton about leadership dynamics and performance, and there were two powerful catchphrases of his that left an indelible impression on me, particularly as it relates to sales leadership.

The first phrase was: *"As goes the leader, so goes the organization."* Those are powerful and profound words. I feel no need to offer editorial comments. Read them again and picture any organization and its leader that come to mind. As goes the leader, so goes the organization. Pretty much says it all, doesn't it?

The other expression that stuck with me is even more applicable to sales management: *"The level of the team rarely, if ever, exceeds the level of the leader."* Let that sink in. Just think about the implications.

How many zillions of dollars are spent on sales training to improve the effectiveness of salespeople, but how little time and money are invested to shore up the leader of those sales teams? Why do some companies simply take it for granted that sales managers know how to lead? And how about smaller organizations, where the founder or president who's a techie, engineer, designer, or accountant by background leads the sales team even though he or she is admittedly ignorant about creating a healthy sales culture, selecting and managing sales talent, or helping to shape sales processes? And if leading the team is the single most important function of the person in charge of sales, why do many larger companies bury that person with so much non-sales leadership work? If we agree it is true that the level of the team will not likely exceed the level of the leader, doesn't it become obvious that to increase sales performance we must increase our sales leader's acumen?

And that is exactly why over the past few years I've intentionally shifted the focus of my consulting practice to offering blunt, practical sales management help to senior executives and sales leaders. Sure, I am still über passionate about new business development, and I am constantly asked to coach and speak on topics from *New Sales. Simplified.* But the cold hard truth is that unless we raise the game of those individuals leading sales organizations, whether as senior executives or frontline sales managers, we won't be making a sustainable impact on sales performance. That fact is what compelled me to write this book. So let's dive into some blunt truth from the front lines and look at many of the reasons sales team are not succeeding at the level they should be.

CHAPTER 2

A Sales Culture Without Goals Is a Sales Culture Without Results

I was kicking off a pretty significant engagement with a good size privately/family-held business in a neighboring state. You'll hear more about this company in subsequent chapters because this was an engagement that I'll never forget—the kind that offered so much fodder for this book that it prompted me to write down the stories as they were happening. They were just too good not to use. The company's vice president of sales was a bright, likable, engaging young man with lots of energy and a deep understanding of the highly technical business. It had been about a year since he was promoted from his regional territory manager sales position to head of sales. He and I actually had struck up a relationship online, mostly via Twitter, and ended up having lunch when he was passing through St. Louis on business.

The company's business was actually pretty darn healthy because it had done an excellent job growing the top line by cross-selling new products and penetrating deeper into existing customers. But its new business development effort was rather anemic. The sales reports they shared with me demonstrated that almost *all* growth was a result of expansion within current accounts. That spoke well of the company's ability to deliver value and manage relationships but not so well about its ability to open new accounts.

After a lengthy process that involved several long phone calls in which the high-ego, rather controlling founder/CEO did most of the talking (telling), and a full day in the boardroom with the executive committee followed by more phone conversations with the CFO, they agreed to hire me. For the record, that was about as much effort ever required on my part to win a new client. Little did I know that the fun was just getting started!

My assignment had two main objectives: First, to help inspire, focus, and equip the sales team to effectively hunt for net new business. And second, to serve as coach to the vice president of sales and help solidify his framework for leading the sales effort.

I flew in for my first day of consulting, and the very first meeting was with the young gun vice president of sales. He was well prepared and ready with all kinds of data and reports. He had even created an iPad app for his sales team that was very useful. I was truly looking forward to working with this guy because he was hungry, thoughtful, and confident—which is a pretty good trio of attributes. After visiting for a few minutes, I prefaced my first question with a statement sounding something like this: "So sales are decent, but we've really struggled to open new customers. Sounds like everyone believes there are a good number of potential major prospects out there that look a lot like some of our best customers, yes?" He concurred. So I said, "All right then, let's begin with this: What are each of your people's individual goals for acquiring new customers? And can you show me how you're measuring and reporting their progress against those goals?"

Silence. Crickets. Nada. After alternating between looking at me quietly and staring down at his notepad for a few seconds, he shook his head and then admitted that his team didn't have individual goals for new account acquisition, and there were no reports to share with me. So I smiled real big (like I'm doing now writing this) and said in a reassuring voice, "Very well. Now we know where to start!"

Goals and Results Go Hand in Glove

From my very first job out of college, it was always stressed that business was about hitting numbers and achieving goals. Period. No matter what the specific job, the yardstick by which you were judged was the actual results you achieved versus your goal. Not exactly a novel concept.

And this *truth* was driven home even more once I moved into sales. So much so, that one of my great sales managers regularly used this phrase: "*In sales, results are everything, and they do not lie.*"

Since the beginning of time, healthy sales organizations have regularly published and distributed sales reports and rankings. Sales versus Last Year. Sales versus Quota for the Month. Sales versus Goal Year-to-Date. Stack Rank of Salespeople by Percentage Increase over Goal or over Last Year. Number of New Accounts Opened/Acquired Year-to-Date versus Goal. Percent of Annual Goal Achieved. And so on.

This practice was never considered abusive, never challenged as not being politically correct, never viewed as some archaic methodology. Publishing sales results was a way of life, a simple reflection of important realities: first, that sales is, in fact, all about results; and second, that by nature, salespeople are not only results-focused but also competitive. The very act of articulating goals, tracking results against those goals, and publishing the results along with a relative ranking of sales team members' performance was considered good sales management. How else would you know how the team and each member are performing? What better way to motivate the team, recognize top performers, and create pressure on those who aren't producing? And all of that could be accomplished without raising a voice, berating people in a high-pressure team meeting, flailing arms, using foul language, or threatening anybody. Plus, it worked!

Yet, over the past few years, I've observed more and more organizations getting away from publishing and widely distributing sales reports. What the heck happened to cause this?

Well, one thing that happened was 2009. The bursting of the real estate bubble that caused the financial markets meltdown of late 2008 pretty much derailed most of industrial American business in the following year. Oh yeah, and concurrently there was this little thing called the European Debt Crisis creating its own havoc for global businesses as well. Many manufacturers, heavy equipment producers, and industrial distributors were off 40 to 50 percent or more! And many marketing companies were completely wiped out as their clients cut as much spending as possible. About one-third of the advertising agencies that my employer at the time served folded their tents. The combination of the financial meltdown and the social media revolution sent cataclysmic waves crashing through the marketing world.

While I didn't recognize it at the time, over the past few years, as I've consulted a good number of both industrial and marketing-type companies that survived 2009 and lived to talk about it, an interesting sales management trend emerged. Many of these companies did an incredible job weathering the severe storm I just described. They cut everything they could to stay afloat. And in order to protect and keep their best talent during the downturn, most completely did away with any form of keeping their sales teams and salespeople accountable for results. The harsh reality was that their markets and customers were off significantly and there wasn't much that could be done about it. As a result, many companies adopted a paternalistic approach toward their best salespeople. They changed pay plans—moving away from pay-for-performance to a higher percentage of fixed compensation. And I've personally observed a whole bunch of businesses that simply stopped publishing depressing sales reports and holding salespeople accountable for hitting goals. With the market in what felt like free fall, how could you blame them? I certainly can't.

But there's one very big *but* to this whole scenario: 2009 was a long time ago! If you're reading or listening to this book right now, it's been at least six years. And in almost every one of these industries mentioned above, there has been an incredibly strong rebound in business. The major stock market indexes have more than doubled. The financial meltdown is getting smaller and smaller in our rearview mirrors. Yet, I continue to observe companies that have not returned to managing their sales organizations the way they used to prior to 2009! Honestly, too many executives and sales managers appear to have forgotten about the importance of goals and accountability for sales teams. Oh, they want the sales results and will complain about not getting them. But many remain slow to create a culture with greater visibility, widely distributed sales reports, and a relentless focus on goals.

Salespeople Are Not Paid by the Hour for Good Reason

Sales is a somewhat unusual job. Salespeople are not paid by the hour, or measured by the quantity of "work" they do. Quite simply, the job of sales is to produce results. And by *results*, I specifically mean to increase revenue, grow the top line, acquire new customers, and net new pieces of business.

What drives me bananas is something that is particularly prevalent in smaller organizations, especially where the founder runs the company as CEO or has a heavy hand in sales management. More often than you'd believe, I face down these controlling CEOs who are more concerned about a salesperson's activity level than whether he is hitting his numbers. These micromanagers' report of choice is the call report, not the monthly or quarterly sales report. That's right. I'm telling you there are chief executives and owners of companies creating a sales culture where producers are not judged on *production versus the goal* but on *activity*. These executives would rather read details about what took place on sales calls and how many customers the salesperson is seeing than dive into actual sales results or opportunities in the pipeline. This is wrong and self-defeating on so many levels, which I'll unpack further in subsequent chapters.

Let me drive home the main point of this chapter right here: You cannot build a sustainable productive, healthy sales culture without a laser focus on goals and results. And that's especially true if you want to maintain a high level of sales talent within the organization. A-players want to be pushed, expect to held accountable for exceeding goals, and won't tolerate being micromanaged.

Before moving on, let me ask: Are the goals of your sales team and each member of it clear? Do all members of your sales team understand what is expected of them and how they'll be evaluated? What processes are in place to monitor progress against specific goals? How are you creating a results-focused culture in your organization?

CHAPTER 3

You Can't Effectively Run a Sales Team when You're Buried in Crap

Be forewarned. I'm a rather emotional guy, and after reviewing my notes for this chapter, I am already angry! The barbs that follow are directed squarely at the senior executive to whom the sales manager reports. But before I begin the tirade, allow me to let you in on one of the dirty little secrets of my consulting practice.

It's Not Rocket Science: Little Effort = Little Results

I get brought into all kinds of companies to help improve the sales effort. On the rare occasion, senior leadership at a high-growth company with a very healthy sales organization will bring me in to help them get to the next level. That's truly a joy and a treat. But as I mentioned, it's also pretty darn rare. Typically, I'm engaged when the sales team isn't working the way it's supposed to; results aren't what they should be—particularly when it comes to bringing in new business—

or sales management is stuck and seeking an infusion of energy, along with a fresh perspective and outside ideas.

Regardless of the size of the company, industry, or even type of sales role, do you know what I *almost always* find? (The only reason I say *almost* is because I've taught my kids that whenever you say *always* or *never* you're probably not telling the truth.) The dirty little secret of this highly paid consultant is that with almost every sales team I've worked who struggle to develop more new business, from SAP consulting firms to printing companies, from OEM truck manufacturers to mortgage lenders, from a highly respected defense contractor to a software company, one of the main causes of underperformance is that the very people charged with selling new pieces of business and acquiring new clients spend a surprisingly low percentage of their time selling new business.

That's it. The secret is out. No matter how complex the business, how tenured the reps, how long the sales cycle, how compelling their sales story, or how well they conduct sales calls, make presentations, or tailor proposals, one of the biggest culprits detracting from sales performance is that salespeople forget their primary job. Quite simply, they get all caught up in doing all kinds of seemingly important activities: playing corporate ambassador, safety committee member, customer service advocate, delivery boy, assistant to the operations manager. You get the point. Salespeople regularly fall short of delivering their numbers because *Little Effort = Little Results.* It's not that they're not working. They're just working on the wrong things.

So why take all this space to expound on why salespeople fail when this chapter is supposedly about companies burying the sales manager? Because sales managers commit the very same sins, but with one huge difference: While salespeople *choose* to take their eye off the new business development ball and are often happily distracted from their primary job, in most cases, sales managers are typically kept from doing their primary job and highest-value activities because their company buries them with an unimaginable amount of crap that has little to do with leading the sales team or driving revenue!

Senior Executives Divert and Distract Sales Managers from Their Most Important Job

As mentioned in Chapter 1, the sales manager's role is already hard enough. People and projects incessantly vie for the manager's time and attention. This happens even though the sales manager is the key leverage point in the organization to drive sales success. Somehow it has become permissible, even fashionable, to pile a large load of non-revenue-driving tasks and responsibilities on this person as well.

I recently facilitated a two-day sales management retreat for a large national client. About two dozen sales managers came to the headquarters city and joined members of the company's executive team. I split up the two days pretty evenly between sessions covering the "Essentials of Sales Leadership" (presented in Part Two of this book), and "Train the Trainer" sessions tackling the critical elements of my New Sales Driver framework from *New Sales. Simplified.* Prior to the retreat, I did some field coaching in several of the client's markets so I had a decent feel for the load these sales managers carried, along with the significant pressure being applied from the executive committee.

During the first day of the retreat I sensed something was amiss. While the managers were intellectually assenting to the sales leadership principles I was espousing, I could tell they weren't truly buying in. In other words, they believed that what I was preaching was true, but they were not reacting like sales managers usually do when I share this content.

On the second day, I set aside time for a closed-door session with just the sales managers. Within a minute of the executive team leaving the room the twenty-five of us were seated informally in a circle. By this point they knew enough about me to understand that things were about to get very real. You could visibly see the angst on several managers' faces. I took a deep breath and exhaled loud enough for everyone to know that I was tracking with them emotionally. I then asked two questions that opened the flood gates:

1. What the heck is going on?

2. And how much worse is it than I think it is?

Voices rose. Expletives flew. Tears flowed. What they described sounded more like *Mission Impossible* than sales management. Along with the tremendous pressure applied from the senior executives (trying to appease their overly involved private equity group owners), these "sales" managers were subject to burdens and expectations that were nearly unbelievable. In one region, the maintenance staff was short-handed, so the sales manager was asked to physically prep the facility for arriving clients. In another, the local executive insisted that the sales manager regularly participate in employee appreciation events, even though they conflicted with her own sales management responsibilities. Another manager decried the fact that when the main incoming phone line was busy or went unanswered, calls would roll over to his number. Several managers were working seven days a week in an effort just to keep up with the litany of tasks. I could fill a few pages with what I heard, but the point has been made. This company, whether intentionally or accidentally, was burying its sales managers to the point of utter exasperation.

I wish the preceding scenario was uncommon, but unfortunately it seems to be the norm in many businesses today. Last year I was hired by an industrial manufacturing company with a strong anti-sales culture. The COO brought me in to look at the sales process, help create a more proactive sales approach for the regional sales managers (who fancied themselves as "sales engineers" as opposed to salespeople), and personally coach the director of sales on sales leadership. Due to aggressive cost cutting, the company was profitable despite flat sales resulting from a protracted slowdown in that particular space, the sales team's lack of leadership, and its reactive, pessimistic mode of operating.

The COO warned me going into the assignment that I likely wouldn't see much good sales management behavior in place because it was widely agreed that the director of sales was overwhelmed. The COO was correct. It was even a challenge scheduling my first coaching session with the director. That should have been a clue to the two dominant issues I quickly uncovered. First, this long-time employee had pretty close to zero interest in being coached—by anyone, let alone by me. And second, to say that this poor man was overwhelmed would be the sales management understatement of the century! He was underwater, breathing through a straw in the midst of a tsunami.

For the first half-hour, sitting in the director's impressive, glass-enclosed office, I just listened. He provided a history lesson about the company's sales management failures over the past fifteen years. He then told me about the various types of meetings he was required to attend on a regular basis. The Production Planning Meeting. The Product Development Meeting. The New Strategy Meeting. The Executive Committee Meeting. The S & OP Meeting. There were more, but I stopped writing them down. When I asked to see his actual calendar, he smiled and gladly walked me over to his desk. What I saw was unfathomable. There was practically no open space, and that's not because he was time-blocking his high-value activities. All of a sudden, the bizarre placard on the wall in the company's men's restroom started to make sense to me.

"IT IS AGAINST COUNTY, STATE & FEDERAL REGULATIONS TO CONSUME EITHER FOOD OR BEVERAGES IN A RESTROOM AREA. WE ASK YOUR COOPERATION IN OBSERVING THESE REGULATIONS."

I kid you not. Word for word, that was on the wall in the men's room. It was so beyond the pale that I snapped a picture and tweeted it (August 14, 2013, if you want to check my Twitter stream).

Was it in the realm of possibility that this company's managers were so over-burdened that they were trying to combine their lunch and pee break into one event? You can't make this stuff up. Another reason I love consulting!

During the second half-hour of this initial sales management coaching session, I began asking the director a few basic questions to get a handle on how he was (wasn't) leading the sales organization:

> *Me:* Tell me how often you get out in the field to spend a day with one of your people.
>
> *Director:* I don't.
>
> *Me:* Let's talk about accountability for members of the sales team. When do you have one-to-one conversations to review sales results with the salespeople?
>
> *Director:* I don't.
>
> *Me:* Okay. How about pipeline reviews, where you go over existing opportunities and what's been added to the pipeline recently?
>
> *Director:* Nope.
>
> *Me:* When are you doing team conference calls?
>
> *Director:* I'm not.
>
> *Me:* How certain are you about team members' level of activity or that they're even targeting the right customers and prospects?

He didn't need to answer. We both knew that we found the problem in our first hour together.

But let me very blunt and very clear here. There was a lot of leadership sin to go around. Yes, clearly this head of sales was confused about his priorities. And he certainly was not taking ownership of his team, his calendar, or sales results. However, and I mean a big however, before throwing any more stones at this faithful, hard-working, long-tenured employee (who happened to be in the wrong job at the wrong time), let's take just a quick look at the situation created for him.

The director had twenty-two direct reports, fifteen of whom were the regional salespeople. The other seven were in support roles: service and marketing. He had no administrative assistance. The company mandated his attendance at all those non-sales management meetings mentioned previously. I also remember the director of sales sharing that he was receiving in excess of 200 emails per day—many which did indeed require his response. In reality, he could've worked 60 hours per week in 100 percent reactive mode and still not have been able to handle all the work being put on his plate, let alone get to the proactive sales leadership priorities I was hired to help him master.

What a disaster. But don't think for a minute these two examples are extraordinary. They're not. I could regale you with stories that would make you both laugh and cry. There's the suffering senior vice president of a major bank who was being evaluated on how her team scored in eighteen categories. That's right: eighteen. My consulting partner at the time looked at her and quizzically asked, "Are you telling me that your company has given you eighteen separate goals and *all* of these are *priorities?*" She offered a huge smile, admitting how ludicrous it was, and replied, "Yes, I have been instructed that each and every one of these eighteen areas on my scorecard is a top priority." What idiots run that company! The only solace in the story is that the clown CEO of the bank was finally tossed out following the discovery that he was less than forthright in some of his dealings during the financial meltdown.

Diverting and distracting the sales manager is a problem of epidemic proportions, and companies are reaping the consequences for what they've sown. They are losing out on sales and they're losing key talent, too. A very big part of the reason I walked away from two high-end sales executive positions and ultimately returned to consulting is because of how little of my time and attention I was able to spend doing what I love: driving revenue. Whether it was the customer service rep giving out my cell phone number because she was told that "all problems go to the sales manager," or, at my last employer, where it had become a game to see how many times a week the CEO could gather executives in the conference room, companies love to bury the sales manager with all kinds of crap and then complain that they're not leading the sales team well.

I would challenge senior executives to take a hard look at the burden they're placing on sales managers. And I specifically ask them to compare the amount time their "sales leaders" spend playing assistant general manager, customer service agent, errand boy, email slave, and committee member versus the amount of time dedicated to the high-value, revenue-driving activities described in Part Two.

CHAPTER 4

Playing CRM Desk Jockey Does Not Equate to Sales Leadership

There is no more ubiquitous sales management tool over the past decade than the customer relationship management (CRM) system. CRMs come in all shapes and sizes, from companies new and old, big and small. None is more widely recognized, talked about, accepted as the *standard*, and loved and hated than the 1,600-pound gorilla in the space, salesforce.com.

I give "Salesforce," as the entire sales world calls it, tons of credit. From the company's fearless leader, Marc Benioff, to its widely read blog, to the annual Dreamforce Conference, which draws 140,000 to San Francisco each fall, to its comprehensive robust platform, Salesforce is to CRMs what Kleenex is to facial tissue—or pretty darn close! And as incredibly valuable as it is for a sales leader and sales team to have such a powerful system to enter, track, and report sales opportunities that also allows you to communicate about and with prospective and current customers, it's still just a piece of software. Yes, I just wrote that. We'll have to see if

Salesforce revokes my guest blogger status once this book is out. And this piece of software, albeit wonderful and powerful, has caused a dramatic, and not necessarily positive, shift in where many sales managers focus their energy and attention.

Salesforce.com Will Fix a Broken Sales Organization Just Like Having Kids Will Fix a Bad Marriage

Earlier this year I was having lunch with the president of a midsize local (St. Louis) company whose sales team was not firing on all cylinders. I'm pretty familiar with this organization and have relationships with a handful of key employees. The company's sales team is disjointed, lacking clarity on which markets to pursue and how to pursue them. There are significant challenges with the company's value proposition, sales process, and compensation plan. Morale is not great (no surprise), and sales management is inconsistent in its approach. Aside from that, the sales organization runs like a well-oiled machine ☺.

The president shared with great excitement that the company had just committed to adopt salesforce.com, and he began to tell me how this would be *the fix* for much of what was wrong with the sales effort. I smiled politely, mentioned that it was a big commitment for his company, and that I hoped it would pay dividends. I bit my tongue to prevent me from telling this wonderful man (not a client) what I was really thinking. What I wanted to scream loud enough to disrupt the whole restaurant was, "Are you crazy? Your whole freakin' sales engine is broken. I know it. You know it. Everyone knows it. Installing a CRM without addressing the many underlying issues and root causes of your sales problems is akin to a couple with a marriage on the rocks deciding to have children thinking that will save their relationship!" Having children adds stress and exposes weaknesses in your marriage. A CRM can be a wonderful tool, but it doesn't have supernatural healing powers, fold your laundry, or make customers run to your doorstep with cash in hand.

Confused Managers Track, Evaluate, and Reinforce the Wrong Behaviors

While CRM systems can, and often do, bring many benefits to both management and salespeople alike, they unfortunately also create their own set of problems. One of the most common (and amusing) changes I observe is that sales managers become CRM jockeys with their heads constantly buried in CRM screens.

It's almost as if CRM adoption causes sales managers to change how they see their job. I can't decipher whether it's because of the pressure managers feel to rationalize their decision to purchase the system (in smaller organizations) or whether they're afraid of being called out by senior management (in larger companies) who made the significant investment. In both cases, I see many sales managers who become obsessed with the sales team religiously updating activity and opportunities in the system.

In and of itself, enforcing CRM compliance across the sales organization isn't a bad thing at all. In fact, it's essential. But the way it plays out in the real world is where it gets dysfunctional. The sales manager who develops OCD around his new CRM begins sending really weird and unhelpful messages to his team. Without actually saying the words, the CRM-addicted manager continually preaching about the need to keep the CRM updated is communicating that it is more important to enter tasks and opportunities swiftly and properly than it is to actually move sales opportunities forward and close deals.

You may snicker reading that assertion, believing it's absurd. Surely, you might think, there isn't an executive or sales manager on the planet who believes that it's more important to keep CRM data fresh and clean than it is to actually sell something. That may be true, but many sales executives' words and actions belie that fact. I've consulted for organizations where members of the sales team would sacrifice putting time, energy, and creativity into advancing significant sales opportunities because they were behind updating tasks in Salesforce. Said differently, these salespeople were making a conscious choice to complete administrative tasks rather than actually selling because they worked under a management philosophy where the consequences were harsher for not updating the CRM than for missing sales goals.

Email and the CRM Are Not Replacements for Personal Leadership

We are now experiencing a new breed of sales managers who were raised in the era of email and CRM systems. Many in this generation of "leaders" did not have the benefit of being mentored by seasoned sales managers, who back in the day not only didn't have these wonderful high-tech tools, but saw it as *their personal responsibility* to develop the sales skills of their team members. If old-time (mid-1990s and earlier) sales managers wanted to evaluate how a salesperson sold—i.e., opened a dialogue, conducted an initial sales call, advanced an opportunity, built consensus, delivered a presentation, handled difficult buyers, etc.—that manager would go into *the field* and actually get in the salesperson's car. Scandalous, I know.

It's beyond comprehension how it has become the norm today to judge a salesperson's ability by solely overanalyzing each of his deals and what percentage of opportunities advance from stage to stage in the CRM. It's as if we've decided to replace true sales experts with quantitative mutual fund managers. Just stick the manager behind a large screen with lots and lots of data under the guise that if she stares at it long enough she'll figure out which stocks to buy . . . I mean which salespeople can sell.

A chapter picking on sales managers for morphing into desk jockeys would not be complete with addressing another huge leadership issue: email. Maybe I missed the memo on this, or possibly the decree was buried on page 2,344 in the Affordable Care Act legislation. But when did it become acceptable to manage people who manage people and relationships via email? Please reread that last question slowly to truly ponder what I am asking here.

We've got salespeople on the front lines (in various capacities from territory managers to hunters to inside salespeople) who live and die based on their ability to connect with people relationally. All these attributes and behaviors—EQ, empathy, being a good listener, resilience, enthusiasm, and the ability to engage in productive dialogue— are critical for them to be successful. Yet somehow, some way, we've arrived at the place where it's acceptable for the people managing these salespeople to do so via email? We've got sales managers emailing either individual reps or the entire team on a regular basis. "I need this. I need that. Where are you on this deal? You're behind; are you going to hit your number this month?" If I showed you some of the emails forwarded to me by salespeople you'd cringe. You'd be angry. You'd scratch your head. These are emails from desk jockey sales managers who spend almost no time face-to-face with their people. Emails with threats. Emails sent on Sunday mornings asking for an immediate reply. Emails asking for status updates. And of course, emails with harsh words about overdue tasks in the CRM. Again, this is all one-way communication from a manager who likely isn't meeting one-on-one regularly with his people, isn't conducting productive sales team meetings, and certainly isn't spending anywhere near enough time out in the field (or the inside sales office) where the work actually happens.

Could you imagine a Major League Baseball team manager, even one like the Chicago Cubs' Joe Maddon, who's known for his love of stats, probabilities, and sabermetrics, not sitting in the dugout during a game? Not watching players perform with his own eyes? Not being around to offer a word of encouragement or correction on the spot? Not caring whether his players' hearts were engaged? Think about the absurdity of a sports team manager sitting in his office all day (and all night) reviewing reports and data, making lineup decisions based only on what he sees on his screens and exported spreadsheets. And when he had a really important message for his team, firing up his email and firing off a missive to the team complaining about their lousy stats, berating them for lack of hustle and work ethic, and challenging their manhood—all by email! How well do you think that would work?

Newsflash for sales managers: Living with your head buried in CRM screens is not akin to *leading* your sales team. And your ability to craft a high volume of sharply worded emails does not substitute for actually managing the people who work for you.

The CRM Is Supposed to Work for You, Not the Other Way Around

Before moving on, let me make this clear. I'm not anti-CRM. I'm simply sharing what is happening at all kinds of companies using CRM systems. In no way am I opposed to using data to help manage the sales process or people. I have forever preached that *"the math works"* and that a high-frequency sales attack almost always trumps low activity levels. It is essential to monitor key metrics and track opportunities through the pipeline. The cloud-based software and systems available today are incredibly powerful and we'd be foolish not to use them—particularly because there are so many choices making it easier to find the solution that fits an organization's needs well.

But let me make this equally clear. A CRM will not, in and of itself, fix your sales issues. If you're not careful, it will not only create an incredible amount of work (installing it, training people on how to use it, and increasing the administrative burden on managers and reps alike), it also might actually slow your sales effort.

It is not uncommon for me to ask a sales manager or executive for details about a particular sales opportunity or if I can see a certain sales report and get this answer: "We don't have that module yet." Or, "We only purchased the base version so we don't have that functionality." Or, "I think that information is available, but we haven't figured out how to retrieve it in a usable format." Oh my.

We all know that salespeople love to whine and bitch, particularly when asked to incorporate something new into their routine. So it's pretty common to get an earful from sales team members about the (in)effectiveness and burden of their new CRM. Sometimes, it's exactly that—just bitching for the sake of being heard. But often, their beefs are legit: Cumbersome systems. Predetermined stages of the sales cycle that don't align well with their reality in the field. Difficulty making their legacy methods play nicely with the new system. Hours spent entering information. Inability to get the desired info at the desired time. And maybe the most frustrating beef of all, getting asked to provide information again that had already been entered into the CRM because someone in management can't get what he wants so he asks for it in a different format!

Hearing similar complaints over and over and over again prompted me to start asking this question: *Is your CRM working for you or are you working for it?* Unfortunately, more often than not, it's the latter. And that's a problem.

CHAPTER 5

You Can Manage, You Can Sell, but You Can't Do Both at Once

People do crazy things in the name of efficiency. Just look at all the idiots driving on our busy roads while staring down at their phones. It's insanity! The lure of multitasking is quite seductive. Requiring key employees "to do more with less" is as fashionable now as it has ever been—particularly during periods of economic contraction. Under the banner of multitasking with the mission of being as *lean* as possible, many companies are making the serious mistake of asking their part-time "sales manager" to both carry a personal quota/sales goal and lead/manage the sales team. That decision may not create the life-safety risk that texting while driving does, but it certainly can destroy sales momentum and the health of the sales force.

I'm all for attempts to be as efficient as possible, and I am in no way in favor of a bloated management structure. In fact, with several small-company clients over the past few years, I've actually argued against adding a full-time sales manager because of the cost and risk involved. However, even in those cases, I have never been in favor of deploying what I refer to as the "player-coach" sales manager who sells part time and manages part time. Why never? Because I've *never* seen it work, and there are significant reasons why.

The Sales Manager and Salesperson Roles Could Not Be More Different

This may sound like an extreme statement, but I don't mean it to be. There is almost nothing similar about being a sales manager and being an individual producer in a sales role. Almost nothing. I thought I understood this principle, at least in theory. But it wasn't until I was tasked with serving as a player-coach selling sales manager that the magnitude of the difference between these two roles crystallized for me.

The successful individual sales producer wins by being as selfish as possible with her time. The more often the salesperson stays away from team members and distractions, puts her phone on Do Not Disturb (DND), closes her door, or chooses to work for a few hours from the local Panera Bread café, the more productive she'll likely be. In general, top producers in sales tend to exhibit a characteristic I've come to describe as being *selfishly productive*. The seller who best blocks out the rest of the world, who maintains obsessive control of her calendar, who masters focusing solely on her own highest-value revenue-producing activities, who isn't known for being a "team player," and who is not interested in playing good corporate citizen or *helping* everyone around her, is typically a highly effective seller who ends up on top of the sales rankings. Contrary to popular opinion, being selfish is not bad at all. In fact, for an individual contributor salesperson, it is a highly desirable trait and a survival skill, particularly in today's crazed corporate environment where everyone is looking to put meetings on your calendar and take you away from your primary responsibilities!

Now let's switch gears and look at the sales manager's role and responsibilities. How well would it work to have a sales manager who kept her office phone on DND and declined almost every incoming call to her mobile phone? Do we want a sales manager who closes her office door, is concerned only about herself, and is for the most part inaccessible? No, of course not. The successful sales manager doesn't win on her own; she wins *through* her people by helping them succeed.

Think about other key sales management responsibilities: Leading team meetings. Developing talent. Encouraging hearts. Removing obstacles. Coaching others. Challenging data, false assumptions, wrong attitudes, and complacency. Pushing for more. Putting the needs of your team members ahead of your own. Hmmm. Just reading that list again reminds me why it is often so difficult to transition from being a top producer in sales into a sales management role. Aside from the word *sales*, there is truly almost nothing similar about the positions. And that doesn't even begin to touch on corporate responsibilities like participating on the executive committee, dealing with human resources compliance issues, expense management, recruiting, and all the other burdens placed on the sales manager.

Again, I knew these facts intellectually. But it wasn't until I assumed a sales leadership role at a company in addition to serving as sales hunter in a new business development capacity that I really came to understand how impossible it was to effectively do both jobs simultaneously. As much as I knew about both sales and sales management, I could not find a way to perform both functions well. It was impossible to gracefully transition back and forth between these roles with their opposing demands. How do you jump from playing selfish individual producer one minute to being a fully accessible manager the next without becoming a total schizophrenic? How do you laser focus on personally developing new business (in and of itself an incredibly challenging position requiring a seller's full devotion) and yet at the same time concern yourself with the heart engagement of the people on your team? How do you create space in your brain to worry about others' results when you're under extreme pressure (and rewarded) to achieve your own personal sales goals?

If you're currently using a selling–sales manager model you may not like my blunt, simple answer to these questions. The hard truth is that you don't and you can't. The model does not work. It's an untenable position. and that's the reason so few businesses (and sports teams) deploy it. As former Chicago Bears Super Bowl–winning coach and current ESPN analyst Mike Ditka will often say, "Players play and coaches coach—and that's all there is to it."

I consulted for three very different organizations in the past year that deployed some form of the player-coach selling manager dual role—a large mortgage lender, a heavy equipment distributor, and an IT services company. All three were sales management disasters. In one, the selling managers also happened to be the top producers at the company. Ninety-five percent of their energy and time was dedicated to their own production. These "managers" pretty much abdicated all management responsibility in the hopes that their people would simply manage themselves. In the second company, the sales manager was a recently promoted top producer with no management experience. Despite the promotion to sales management, his company leadership asked him to continue *carrying a bag*, prospecting major accounts, and managing key customer relationships. Because personal selling was his comfort zone and a security blanket, that's what he defaulted to—shying away from asserting himself as the team leader and avoiding the necessary hard conversations with his seasoned reps. In essence, he was simply acting as another salesperson, not providing any meaningful leadership at all. So what was the point of promoting him in the first place? Not only didn't the company fill its sales management vacuum, but there was also tension created because several sales veterans perceived that they were now competing with their manager.

It's Deadly when Managers Compete with Their Own People

The situation in the third organization perfectly illustrated how the player-coach selling manager role can create mistrust and bad feelings across the sales organization. At this company, the sales manager had no shame in cherry-picking the best leads and sales opportunities for himself! The very person who was supposed to be leading the team was using his advantageous position to effectively *steal* from his teammates. In essence, the manager had become a threat, a formidable internal competitor.

Aren't trust and integrity two of the most important characteristics we seek in our leaders? How in the world can you build trust in your sales organization when the guy in charge is effectively taking food off the table of the people entrusted to him? It doesn't take much to see how the health of an entire sales team can be destroyed in a New York minute in situations like this.

I understand that it's tempting to ask a key employee to handle more than one role, but just like sports teams abandoning the notion of the player-coach position, so must sales organizations. There is no place for a selling manager because the dangers are too great and the two roles are incompatible. If a smaller company can't afford a dedicated manager, I'd rather see the president or another key executive (as long as it's not the head of operations—see Chapter 7) serve in a part-time sales management capacity. While that is not an ideal situation, it certainly is preferable to having a schizophrenic player-coach selling manager whose conflict of interests may sabotage the health of the entire team.

CHAPTER 6

A Sales Manager Either Wants to Make Heroes or Be the Hero

In late 2010, the executive team from my last employer attended a valuable conference where Liz Wiseman was one of the main speakers. Wiseman had just released a powerful book titled *Multipliers: How the Best Leaders Make Everyone Smarter* (New York: HarperBusiness, 2010), which became a *Wall Street Journal* bestseller. To say that her presentation made a huge impact on my colleagues and me would be a severe understatement. Several of us immediately read her book and began openly discussing its major themes. Not only did this help us better articulate the frustration of working with our CEO, who was the poster child for one of the management styles described by Wiseman, it also provided me a wonderful word picture to describe a very common sin in sales managers.

There Are Two Very Different Approaches to Leading

The extensive research done for *Multipliers* concluded that there are essentially two broad categories of leaders—those who are "Multipliers" and those who are "Diminishers." The Multiplier makes everyone around him better, smarter, and more productive. He challenges those on his team to raise their game. He asks hard questions. He paints the big picture and shares what needs to be accomplished. He multiplies his effectiveness and that of his team by engaging their hearts and minds. Everyone wants to work for a multiplier, and Wiseman's book cites example of how employees will run through, around, and over walls to achieve victory for this style of leader.

The Diminisher takes a very different approach that produces an opposite effect. He comes into the meeting with all the answers and makes sure everyone knows he's the smartest guy in the room. Instead of engaging his people's passion and intellect by pointing to the hill they need to conquer and asking them to give their best to make it happen, he not only *tells* them what to do, but also *how* they should do it! He's the genius and wants to be the hero of every story. He drains energy and intelligence from his people and negatively impacts the team's performance. Yuck. Even writing this paragraph produces a visceral reaction as I recall the pain and discouragement of working for this type of leader.

This concept is so powerful yet so easy to grasp that I'm confident even reading this now you are dividing managers and executives you know into these two categories. So let's apply this profound truth to sales management. In her book, Wiseman challenges leaders to ask themselves this provocative question: Are you a genius or a genius-maker? I've slightly adapted that question to be more specific for sales leaders:

Are you the hero or the hero-maker?

The answer to this question is so important to the health and success of a sales organization that if I was asking you this from the front of the room during a workshop, I'd pause for an uncomfortably long time to let the awkward silence build as you pondered the enormity of your answer. It's that important.

Can I be so bold as to ask you to put aside this book, grab a pen and paper, and write this question at the top of the page: "As the sales team leader, have I been operating and positioning myself as the hero or the hero-maker?" Ponder the question, your mindset, your words, your actions, and how you approach sales opportunities and your people. Please don't shortchange this exercise. What you uncover here may be one of your most important takeaways from *Sales Management. Simplified.*

Welcome back. I only wish we could debrief over a cup of coffee so I could hear your thoughts. I make such a big deal about this point because I've witnessed so many sales managers with a hero complex just waiting for an opportunity to don their superhero leotard and cape so they can swoop in and save the day.

The Sales Manager with a Hero Complex Destroys the Energy of the Team

The sales manager with a hero complex reveals himself in various ways. Early in the sales cycle, we see him play hero on sales calls. Instead of letting the salesperson lead the preparation, plan the strategy, and conduct the meeting, the manager acts like the overzealous flight instructor who plans everything for the student pilot and at the slightest misstep or point of indecision immediately takes control of the airplane. Continuing with the cockpit analogy, this manager isn't content to sit in the right seat and simply play his role during a meeting with a customer or prospect. No, he looks for every opportunity to grab the yoke and call out "my airplane," taking control of the flight. He's quick to figuratively jump into the left seat to run the sales call. He knows he has this habit but covers up for it by telling the salesperson afterward that the opportunity was too important to fumble.

The sales manager with a hero complex will also use the excuse that he wants to "model the way" for salespeople so they can see how it is supposed to be done. Sure, there are times that call for the senior person to jump in or bail out the junior one. But does the baseball manager run out of the dugout to grab the bat from the batter in the middle of an at-bat and jump into the batter's box himself? No, that would be absurd. Beyond being against the rules of the game, that surely isn't the best way to develop a player's skills, is it? We'll dive deeper into the whole topic of sales managers working the field in Chapter 22.

Later in the sales cycle, the hero complex manager will find other opportunities to swoop in and save the day. I've seen sales managers discover a truly hot deal that didn't require their involvement up to that point. Somehow, right before the big deal closes, the manager manages to insert himself into the situation just in time to get his fingerprints on the paperwork. Other managers are masters at finding "flaws" in perfectly fine presentations and proposals. Their hero complex compels them to suggest often unneeded changes—again, so their fingerprints can be seen on the deal. It is laughable.

If those sins aren't bad enough, what's even more sickening is how some managers describe a deal and parcel out the credit following a victory. Whether it's standing up at a big company meeting or talking about the win in front of the executive committee, somehow the sales manager, instead of the salesperson, always ends up as the hero. He's the one who opened the door in the first place. He overcame the prospect's insurmountable objection to alter the course of history. He fixed the awful presentation at the last minute or, even better, flew out to deliver it himself. He resurrected the deal from the dead by jumping in to get it back on track. Hand me the garbage can because I'm getting nauseated reliving these examples.

My former sales manager, Donnie Williams, who later became my consulting partner, taught me a long time ago that sales is as much about the heart as it is about the head. And if there's anything guaranteed to deflate the heart of a salesperson, it is the manager stealing the glory and limelight.

The very best sales managers are Multipliers. They subdue their own egos for the sake of their people. They understand that their mission is to win through their salespeople. They don't micromanage every detail. When necessary, they ask insightful questions that challenge the status quo and a salesperson's approach. Instead of jumping in and taking over at every chance, they look for coaching opportunities. Great sales managers deflect the credit; they don't steal it. And they often jump in front of the bus to protect their people rather than throwing them under it so they look good themselves.

CHAPTER 7

Sales Suffer when the Manager Wears the Fire Chief's Helmet

It's pretty common to see the sales leader play a number of roles. In most cases, I don't think that it is as much due to the hero complex discussed in the previous chapter as it is because sales managers tend to be highly driven and possess useful talents. Most are more than willing to wear a variety of hats and contribute as needed.

Looking for someone to emcee the all-company meeting or serve as host of the annual awards dinner or company holiday party? Who better than the sales leader? The executive retreat is coming up and HR needs someone to lead the team-building exercises? Of course the VP of Sales fits the bill. Honestly, those are great uses for the head of sales to deploy her many talents. But oftentimes, the sales leader's competitive nature and strong desire to solve *all* problems that affect sales get in the way of doing her primary job: leading the sales team.

The Sales Leader Should Not Be Firefighter-in-Chief

It is entertaining to watch sales leaders grab the fire hose and don the firefighter helmet. Many relish the opportunity to jump in and put their strong problem-solving skills to work. They are often very good at attacking problems, even ones only ancillary to sales. The issue, however, is the opportunity cost of having the leader of your forward-deployed special operations forces remove her battle helmet and replace it with one of a firefighter. Sure, your sales leader is a highly valuable resource who may even excel at solving manufacturing or work flow challenges. But that is neither her primary job nor the most valuable use of her time.

In the past few years, I've observed sales managers involved in everything from traveling overseas to source potential new manufacturers to "helping" plant managers plan production. At one client with significant quality issues on a new product, the head of sales was as technically competent as the engineers overseeing quality control. Because this sales executive cared deeply about getting the product right for an important customer, he dove headfirst into problem-solving mode. This was probably driven by a combination of his knowledge about manufacturing, his strong desire to save the customer relationship, and his natural tendency to grab the hose when a fire is burning. By themselves, those aren't bad qualities. In fact, they're admirable. But my issue as the consultant hired to help him improve as the sales team leader was that almost every time I tried to reach him, he was either on a conference call with the engineers and QC folks or working the problem using his own resources. Sure, it was a big issue and there was plenty at stake. But this issue became his main issue, and as time went on during this engagement, his tendency to fight fires became more and more apparent. The bottom line is that while he was certainly helping solve other problems, he was taking his eye off the one ball that the company could not afford him to lose focus on.

There are also many managers of sales organizations who set

40

themselves up as "The Shell Answer Man." If you're too young to know what that means, go Google it, because it's the perfect metaphor for what I'm describing. For inexplicable reasons, the sales manager inserts himself at the crossroads of all sales team communication and serves as the fount of all knowledge. He's the expert on every topic and the go-to resource whenever someone, particularly a salesperson, needs an answer. People are lined up to see him like airplanes stacked up in the sky flying into Chicago O'Hare at 5:00 P.M. Not clear about the suitability of a certain product in a certain application? Call the sales manager. Pricing question? See the sales manager. Problem getting a product delivered to a key customer? Get the sales manager to fight the battle or authorize overtime or expedited shipping. Trying to choose an airline, restaurant, or new smartphone? Go talk to the Sales Manager Answer Man!

When the Same Person Heads Up Sales and Operations

There is another huge issue that often hurts sales results. This particular problem is most prevalent in smaller companies (or divisions) with revenue typically under $50 million. In these situations, it is not uncommon for there to be a general manager who heads up both sales and operations for that division, branch, or company.

Just about every time I run into a struggling sales team where the boss runs both the operations and the sales departments, he defaults to solving operational issues over sales leadership. It might be as simple as the fact that operational challenges tend to be right in front of the manager and urgent, as opposed to sales problems, which are less easily diagnosed and whose consequences won't be felt until the month- or quarter-end sales report gets published.

I was doing a consulting project for a Midwest client that had recently acquired a company in another city (which I won't name to protect the guilty). The CEO engaged me to help change the sales culture and better equip the various sales teams to hunt for new business. The newly acquired company was left to operate as a mostly independent division with its own president and general manager kept in place. This division was given significant growth goals, and the marching orders from the CEO were as clear as day: Sell like madmen; hunt for new customers; make the sales numbers. Period. End of story.

I would make regular visits to the office of this out-of-town division. I'd spend time with the inside sales team, the outside salespeople, the president, and the GM. I would facilitate sales team meetings and also work one-on-one with its various members. After a few trips, the problem with the sales effort became abundantly clear. The people on the sales team weren't acting like salespeople. The general manager had an operational bent, rather than a sales bent, and that bias permeated the sales force.

One day we were in a sales meeting where I was coaching the team on conducting more effective sales calls. The salesperson who managed some of the largest accounts started to play on his phone. At least I thought he was playing. Once it became evident that he was no longer *present* with us, I stopped what I was doing to let the awkward silence build. The salesperson figured out pretty quickly that he was the cause of the silence in the room. He looked up and apologized, and then shared that he was working to get a crew scheduled for a customer's major service the next day. I scratched my head because I was under the impression that this was a *salesperson* and we were in a *sales meeting*. Why was one of my client's most valuable salespeople worried about scheduling service work? The general manager was not in the meeting with us at the time, but I strongly suspect he would've condoned the account manager's choice to work on an operational issue instead of honing his skills.

As I dug deeper into that division, I began to notice more of the same attitude and behavior. The inside sales team was having a difficult time hitting the daily activity goals for outbound calls and emails that everyone agreed were reasonable. Not only were their results nowhere close to plan week after week, but their activity levels made it look like they weren't even trying. I headed back to their office ready to dedicate two full days to work exclusively with the inside sales team. I was bound and determined to figure out what in the world was preventing these sellers from doing their selling. Well, it took about two hours, not two days, to see what was happening. The general manager had tasked the inside sales team with all kinds of non-sales work. The team members were responsible for picking a certain type of custom order from the warehouse that took an inordinate amount of time. They were also charged with managing shipping logistics on international orders. On top of all of that, the customer service reps were offloading a portion of their incoming calls to these inside salespeople. I was relieved that it wasn't laziness or neglect getting in the way of selling. But it was infuriating that the operational-minded GM created a situation where it would be almost impossible for the sales team to hit its aggressive goals. Below are excerpts from a summary I sent to the president and CEO:

> *Said simply, the sales reps (account managers) self-described their roles as very broad, complex, comprehensive "catch-all" positions that included selling new business, maintaining existing business, serving as lead customer service reps on their current accounts, and in some cases, either concerned with scheduling crews or responsible for shipping product....*
>
> *(Name redacted—large account salesperson mentioned above) feels completely responsible for the entire experience of his customers, and he carries the burden of ensuring that service crews are deployed on jobs... he sounds more like an ops guy than a salesperson in his words and expressions. His plate appears very full, and under the current model, it is hard for me to see how he could have success developing new business.*

I could regale you with more stories from this company, but suffice it to say that it was an uphill battle forcing change on this division. Its GM was constantly diving deep into office management and operational issues while either ignoring or working against the new business development sales effort. Having been given a green light from the CEO to boldly confront him, I was ready to take the gloves off and share some blunt truth. When I got to the office to meet the GM early one morning, I found him in the server room holding a handful of Ethernet cables. He shrugged his shoulders and told me that the network was down. What a perfect visual to illustrate my point! I'll never forget the image of him standing there holding those blue cables. And I'll never stop preaching about the dangers of the person heading up operations also leading the sales team.

I have another client with a very different situation but a similar challenge. It is a relatively small company run by a CEO who is truly pro sales and a sales pro himself. The CEO serves as part-time sales manager; I consult him and coach the solid sales team he's built. We are coming off a blowout year, and the sales team is running at full stride. Its members are competent and confident. Momentum is on their side. It's one of those really fun times for me as the consultant when the monkey has clearly shifted from sales' back onto the back of the operations folks. But it's not fun for the operations team, and I can sense the CEO getting tight as his people struggle to produce this giant load of work the sales team has booked.

Donnie Williams, the friend, mentor, and former partner I mentioned earlier, had a great expression when the salespeople would start to let up, fearing that they were overloading the production people. He would say, "Don't ever confuse sales and operations." And I can't remember if this next line was his or mine, but we both used it all the time: "Your job is not to have mercy on operations; your job is to bury the bastards." Just in case you think that was said tongue-in-cheek, be assured it was not. We were dead serious, and I still am! I continually remind executives and salespeople alike that the sales car has only one pedal, and it's the skinny one on the right. Our job as sales leaders is to keep the RPMs up and the sales engine in the power band. Similar to Jim Collins's now famous flywheel analogy from *Good to Great* (New York: HarperBusiness, 2001), it takes a ton of energy to build up sales momentum. The very last thing we want a sales team to do is to take their collective feet off the gas and slow down the car.

I know my CEO client is tempted to rein in the sales team. But he is wise enough to know that is not an option. It took years to build up the new business development momentum they are experiencing, and I give him credit for not applying the brakes, knowing that the current problem beats the heck out of his old problem!

The sales world works a lot better when sales leaders focus on their primary job: leading the sales team and helping to drive revenue.

CHAPTER 8

The Trouble with One-Size-Fits-All Sales Talent Deployment Is That One Size Does Not Fit All

Simple observation: Many sales organizations' *sales problems* are really more of a *talent problem*. It's not just that they don't have enough top producers or true salespeople; it's that they haven't done the hard work to truly define the sales roles in their business.

A salesperson is not a salesperson is not a salesperson. There are as many types of sales roles as there are colors of crayons. The territory manager. The servicer. The inside prospector. The outside big game hunter. The route guy. The sales engineer. The industry specialist. The pure business development person. The merchandiser. The account manager. The retail floor person. The _____.

Beyond the various types of formal sales roles, there are a myriad of talents, preferences, and styles that sellers bring with them to their positions. Some are natural networkers. Others thrive at prospecting. Many are good with transactional-type sales. There are those who master serving existing accounts, and those who aren't the best maintainers but do a heck of a job roaming the halls to meet new people and uncover new opportunities. There are salespeople built to quarterback long-term complex deals that require patience and political deft. There are individuals who are comfortable walking in the back door or leaning over a piece of heavy plant equipment. And for all the talk about selling to the C-Suite, there appears to be only a rare few sellers who can truly hold their own going toe-to-toe with senior executives. And that is why a one-size-fits-all approach to salespeople and sales roles hinders revenue growth.

Sales Role Clarity Is Essential

I decided to walk away from my first consulting business (and partnership with Donnie) after four years. The consulting treadmill wore me down, and the travel demands were taking a toll at a time when my children were at the ages where I felt compelled to be around more. While I had experienced success as the top-producing salesperson in several companies, and had a thrilling run coaching sales teams and consulting executives, I had yet to lead a sales organization. So I left consulting for a season and took a job as the chief sales executive at a $90 million flooring and surface products distributor.

The company was really three companies with three headquarters, three presidents, and three separate sales organizations all loosely held together by a group of corporate executives whose ranks I was joining as head of sales. Sadly, within two hours of my first day on the job I realized that taking it was a mistake. And that was before the owner "took" me out for lunch to welcome me. I say "took" because he invited me but then didn't buy my lunch. I guess he figured he was paying me enough, so there was no reason to show hospitality to his newest corporate executive. It was, by far, the most awkward first day on the job I can remember. Almost every day was painful, but I toughed it out for almost three years because I was learning about sales leadership (the hard way), and the company was in a major transition while the market for its products was in meltdown.

There were some enormous sales challenges at this company, not the least of which was the very wide range of responsibilities and requirements placed on the typical territory salesperson. For perspective, one day a salesperson might be lugging heavy tools and tile samples to spend hours sweating to build a new display, and the next day he might find himself sitting with the owner of a seven-store chain to negotiate terms of a major annual program. It not only made no sense to me, but it also presented a huge compensation problem. How could the same person be expected to be good at such divergent jobs? And where do you find someone happy to play merchandiser on Monday, yet capable of winning a multi-hundred-thousand-dollar deal on Wednesday?

The answer is that you don't. After concluding that this absurd model was preventing us from creating the "World Class Sales Organization" the CEO charged me to build, I did my best to try to convince him that we didn't have one sales job but three completely different jobs requiring different skill sets and very different levels of pay. There was a $30,000 merchandising/service/display-building role, a $75,000 territory manager role, and a $120,000 key account manager role. The truth is that there aren't too many six-figure guys willing to build and dust displays, so we had a very average sales team filled with frustrated people serving in this "tribrid" role, and a frustrated sales executive who won the argument but never got the nod to redefine the roles and redeploy the troops.

Role clarity and talent requirement issues show up in all kinds of businesses. Not long ago, I had a small client with a strong brand, award-winning facility, and well-connected owner-executives. The company's name and logo were everywhere, it had a handful of flagship blue-chip clients, and it invested heavily to regularly advertise in the local business journal as well as sponsor various events and seminars. I was brought in to tune up its new business development effort and inherited two relatively new hires who were charged with hunting for new clients.

After a month it became apparent to me that neither was a very good fit for the role, and I predicted that even with an improved framework and the best coaching I could provide, they likely wouldn't succeed. The two sales guys couldn't have been more different, as were the reasons they both eventually failed. While the company invested significant dollars in its marketing effort, the goal was to increase brand awareness more than it was to create leads. Therefore, the job required the salespeople to self-generate leads and opportunities.

The industry veteran new hire came with a Rolodex of great contacts in the space, but he was unable to use them because he was bound by an iron-clad noncompete agreement. This relationship-style networker-type sales guy was not very interested in prospecting. Sure, once he got face-to-face with a prospective customer, he was solid and possessed good industry knowledge, but he wasn't getting there nearly enough. His pipeline was perpetually weak. The rookie, on the other hand, was eager, coachable, and hungry. He picked up prospecting as fast as anyone I'd coached. He was able to secure discovery meetings, but then he ran into a brick wall because he didn't have the business acumen, experience, or gravitas to continue moving an opportunity forward.

The situation with this company was even more complex than the challenges with the salespeople just described. Over time, I came to understand that the majority of its significant wins came when the senior executives engaged senior executive peers at prospective clients. The sale was often an enterprise-level decision, and the business case to outsource this critical function was appealing to a prospect's senior executives. Therefore, my client's messaging was targeted at reasons why senior executives would want to make this type of move, but, and this is a big *but,* that messaging was not appealing at all to the middle managers the salespeople were targeting. The end result? These two salespeople never had a chance. They were ill-equipped to do their assigned job and completely miscast for the job their company really needed them doing (calling on senior executives).

Be Wary of the Big Reputation, Wily Industry Veteran

If I've seen one company burned by shelling out a large guarantee to bring on a big reputation, veteran salesperson from within her industry, I've seen twenty. The lure is strong. The decision seems like a no-brainer. How could this long-time producer for someone else in your space not hit home runs for your company? Let me count the ways!

Companies I've worked for and companies I've consulted for have made this painful, expensive mistake. Word gets out that one of the top dogs at a competitor or similar company is available. She's been around forever. Everyone has heard her name. She sells three times what your average person does, or so the rumors go. You'd die to have her on your sales team, and after several confidential interviews you are convinced that she'll be able to bring over a decent portion of her current book of business to your place. You convince yourself that she's an expert, the true sales killer you've always wanted. Plus, she's familiar with the industry so there will no learning curve and a lightning fast ramp-up. As I said, it's a no-brainer.

You ruffle some feathers on your existing team by giving her a prime office. Your people already resent her because word got out that you guaranteed so much money in her first year that she'd have to set a Guinness World Record closing deals to pay for herself. And you find yourself deferring to her in sales team meetings because you want everyone to hear from the new expert. If you've lived this scenario before, you're already squirming as you read because you have a good idea how this plays out.

After a few months, your expensive free agent acquisition starts to do her thing and successfully brings over a handful of her past customers. You're happy but also getting anxious because it doesn't look like she is filling her pipeline with opportunities at the rate you expected. Her new business activity just isn't there. You wait another month or so giving your star time to shine, but your anxiety level edges higher as the trickle of customers coming over from her previous employer dries up. And it doesn't look like she's hunting for new business like a sales killer would.

You finally are frustrated or scared enough to initiate a hard conversation. You sit the star down and gently share that you are a little concerned. Of course, you hold back your true feelings because you tell yourself not to deflate the star by communicating a loss of confidence. But you do ask some hard questions and inquire when she is going to spring into action. She responds by citing the challenges she's having with the way your company works and also listing potential deals she's working. You make it clear you need to see more and that you're counting on her to produce big numbers. She says she completely understands and the meeting ends.

This cycle of nonperformance, confusion, and frustration continues for months, the only difference being that these meetings with her become more emotional and more combative because you are acutely aware how much you're paying her each month. Eventually you realize you made a mistake. You're out a lot of cash. Your CFO, who was opposed to the deal from day one, is now asking if you should keep throwing good money after bad, and you can just sense your salespeople thinking "I told you so." But because you've invested so much in this person and she came so highly regarded, you decide that it doesn't make sense to cut your losses yet. So you keep her around another six months hoping and praying she hits the jackpot. Or maybe you decide you've had enough and send her packing. Either way, this *sure thing* turned out to be a bust.

Why did it play out like this? What were the lessons? Why did I feel compelled to drag you through that lengthy chronology? Because it is a great illustration of what happens when sales roles aren't properly defined and management doesn't match appropriate talent and skill sets to those clearly defined roles.

In the disastrous sales star scenario just presented, here are some key puzzle pieces that the executive did not discover until it was too late. Because Sales Star had been with her previous company so long, she was the alpha seller. She received preferential treatment. Sure, back in the early days she'd hunt for business. But it was easy then. The industry was hot and the economy booming. She was younger and hungrier, so she did what she had to. After a couple of years, she became the number one producer. From that point, the company fed her an abundance of great leads. In fact, it not only turned over all the best leads to her but, over time, as other people moved on, the company gave her the very best accounts to manage. So simply due to her seniority and large presence in the company, she was pretty much guaranteed to stay on top of the sales list. The truth is that she hadn't hunted down a new account on her own in over a decade and, on top of that, it became much harder to acquire those mega-clients that made up the bulk of her portfolio. Essentially, Sales Star was living the good life of a tenured professor and making a killing by simply care-taking her cherry account list.

The senior executive got *big eyes* upon learning she was available. He became so enamored with the possibility of luring Sales Star to his company that he didn't bother to ask how she became and stayed the top producer for so long. He had *happy ears* and couldn't discern that she was no longer hungry or interested in the hard work of hunting for fresh game. And maybe worst of all, he never clearly defined and laid out his expectations for how she'd invest her time and truly hunt for new business once coming onboard. Almost none of the recruiting and interviewing rigor that would have been applied for interviewing regular candidates was used with Sales Star. The company paid a heavy price and learned a painful lesson. It's the kind of mistake you make only once.

Farmers and Engineers Often Resist Picking up a Weapon

There is one more critical one-size-fits-all talent issue that drastically hinders sales performance: True sales hunters are a unique and rare breed. The majority of sales teams are composed mostly of farmers (account managers) and engineers (product/service experts). One of the most common causes of sales team underperformance is when companies deploy farmers and engineers in hunting-type sales roles, expecting them to pick up a weapon in search of new prey to kill.

Hunting for new business and acquiring new clients is a very different job from managing existing client relationships. I spend a great deal of my coaching time helping farmer-type salespeople to become more proactive. Yes, you can equip sales farmers with better sales weaponry and coach them how to proactively pursue new business. But the challenge is more complex than simply helping or forcing traditionally reactive sellers to be more proactive. It's a sales DNA thing; we all have different natural tendencies and behavioral styles. And the makeup of successful sales hunters is often the opposite of that of salespeople who thrive as account managers or technical sales experts.

Hunting for new business involves risk, conflict, and rejection. Those three elements are ever-present. The beauty in that? Top sales hunters know and accept the conditions of the role. They are energized by the risk, love the battle, look forward to the conflict, and could not care less about being rejected. But the vast majority of people who gravitate toward account management, sales support, or sales engineer roles are polar opposites. They tend to be uncomfortable with risk, conflict, and rejection. Some are even honest enough to admit that conflict makes them sick. To the highly relational or analytical person, rejection is not just personal, but paralyzing.

It generally doesn't go very well when asking super-relational or super-analytical/technical sellers to pick up a weapon and go on the hunt. Recently I worked with a company whose sales team fancied themselves sales and application engineers. These were technically competent field salespeople. Often they would sell a piece of production equipment to a customer and then come back to install it themselves. These guys (100 percent male sales force) were gearheads and application experts in their space. And while that was a huge advantage when it came to servicing existing customers, it was as big an obstacle when they were challenged from on high to develop new business.

The type of people who gravitate to technical field engineer–type sales positions thrive when machines go down but tend to either panic or hide when asked to find and open new accounts. The more pressure from senior management to find new business, the better these sales engineers get at *finding* service emergencies at the existing customers requiring their immediate attention! I know it's hard to believe, but it was amazing how many machines started going down around their territories that *prevented* these guys from selling new business. Coincidence? I think not.

There is a seasoned sales guru in my town with whom I'll grab coffee about once a year. The last time we met I was sharing about my experience with the flooring distributor and the situation with this client's sales team. My friend smiled and then dropped this pearl of wisdom on me: "Their hunter will kill your farmer every time." He didn't mean it in a violent or morbid sense. He was simply stating what he had observed over three decades: Hunters carry weapons and love to use them. The takeaway: Think carefully before putting account managers in new business development sales roles. And be realistic with your expectations when insisting that your highly relational or highly analytical salespeople pick up a weapon and head out to hunt.

CHAPTER 9

Turning a Blind Eye to the Perennial Underperformer Does More Damage than You Realize

Executives and sales leaders speak often about the importance of accountability in their organizations. But when it comes to maintaining a high-performance culture and a laser focus on results, actions speak much louder than words. Frankly, talk about accountability is cheap—and dangerous. The leader who is constantly preaching about holding people accountable for results and doesn't follow through does more damage than if he hadn't said anything in the first place.

Johnny Never Makes His Numbers

When kicking off a longer-term project with a new client, I'll typically sit down with the senior executive who brought me in to get his take on the members of the sales team. Invariably, he gets around to telling me about Johnny, the perennial underperformer. The dialogue goes something like this:

Exec: I want you to spend extra time with Johnny; he's really struggling.

Me: Tell me what you mean by "struggling."

Exec: He's way behind plan for this quarter (year, decade, etc.), and I'm worried about him. Blah, blah, blah....

Me: When's the last time Johnny had success?

Exec: Long enough ago that I can't remember. Honestly, I am not even sure if he should be in sales.

Me: Tell me more about Johnny's background, temperament, and talents.

Exec: (Lists some milquetoast attributes and says what a good guy he is.)

Me: Let me make sure I have this straight. You've hired me to put a charge into your sales efforts and you want me to spend extra time with Johnny—who hasn't hit quota in so long you can't remember. You're not sure he even belongs in sales. (Give a dramatic pause, raise one eyebrow, and continue with an incredulous tone.) And you now want your highly compensated consultant to assess Johnny and spend extra time coaching him?

Exec: (Gives me a look that he knows where this is going and braces himself for a dose of blunt truth about to come his way.)

Me: I'll tell you what. Let me help you make the decision today that you've been putting off, possibly for years. I don't need to spend any time, let alone extra time, with Johnny. If I were to use the fee you've paid me to work with Johnny, I'd be wasting your money and committing malpractice.

Exec: I know.

Me: There is a 95 percent probability that after I spend time with Johnny I'm going tell you that he is not going to succeed and we need to move him out of the position. So let's not waste any more time on this. Do what you need to do now, and let me focus on people and areas that will move the needle for your sales team.

Exec: (Exhales a sigh of relief and thanks me.)

You would think that type of exchange would be rare, but it's not. What's even more perplexing is when it is the hard-charging, tough-as-nails executive who most needs the mirror held up close to see his blind spot regarding underperformance.

I cannot state this any plainer: Sales. Is. About. Results. Period.

Salespeople are not paid to do *work*, or to be *busy*. The job is to drive revenue—specifically, new revenue. What is surprising is how the same executive who will not tolerate failure from other managers and employees will somehow turn a blind eye to sales failure. Think about it. How many months in a row would you tolerate inaccurate month-end financial reports from your controller or accounting manager? How many times would you allow your shipping clerk to mismark boxes headed to customers before you insisted a change be made? How many projects not completed on time could you stomach before removing a project manager from the role? How many times would you frequent a restaurant with lousy service and subpar food before you stopped going there? So why in the world is it okay for a salesperson to essentially *fail* month after month and quarter after quarter and yet remain in the position?

I understand that many readers will take issue with that last question. They'll say that I'm not familiar with their business. Or they will bemoan their very long sales cycle that makes judging a seller's effectiveness difficult. Others will offer lengthy explanations for how complicated it is to sell their offerings. And still others will simply write me off as a cold-hearted jerk who gets pleasure from tossing out underperformers. Believe me; I get it. I've heard all these reasons, and many more, used as management excuses for being slow to change out talent. But that's really all it is: an excuse. There are various ways to measure sales effectiveness and maintain a performance-driven culture without being an ass, and I offer a specific sales management account-ability progression in Chapter 20 to help.

Everyone Else's Livelihood Is Dependent on Your Sales Team's Success

Not to be dramatic, but is this not true? Is not the very livelihood of every employee in your company dependent upon the success of your sales team? There is no bottom line without a top line. There is no software to code or boxes to pack if your sales team isn't selling. If you fail at sales then there's no quality to control, no product to ship, no customer to service, no revenue to count. Period. Everyone else's paycheck relies on the premise that members of your sales team will do their job and do it well! And that should be reason enough not to tolerate long-term underperformance from salespeople or sales managers.

One Hundred Percent Commission Is Not a Pass to Overlook Failure

Another common excuse for turning a blind eye toward long-term underperformance is tied to a business's compensation model. I dive deeper into compensation in the next chapter, but for now, let me point out a common misconception of business owners and sales leaders who deploy 100 percent commissioned sellers.

In businesses like insurance or mortgage lending, commission-based compensation with no base salary is the norm. The producers, as they're typically called in those businesses, function more like inde-pendent operators than employees. They essentially run their own business, maintain their own "book," pay the majority of their selling expenses, and have no cap on what they can earn. And most owners/partners/branch managers love the model because salespeople who don't produce don't get paid. That's all well and good and makes per-fect sense. However, I've seen multiple instances where leaders at these types of companies completely abdicate management responsibility over low producers. When questioned why they don't hold their bottom people accountable for achieving at least a minimum acceptable level of production, they'll commonly respond by saying they don't care: "Why should I bother to manage them? They're not producing and they're not costing me anything to have them around."

Au contraire! Not costing you anything? You must be kidding. What about the effect on your supposedly *high-performance culture?* The negative vibe that pollutes the office? Sending the message to your whole organization that underproduction is tolerated? And that doesn't even touch on the opportunity cost of keeping people who don't deliver results. Could that desk or cube be put to better use? What about the internal resources that could be redeployed to provide even more support to top producers who know what to do with it? I would argue strenuously that keeping your lowest producers around does *cost* you, even if you're not shelling out commission dollars. In fact, it costs you a lot!

CHAPTER 10

COMPensation and COMPlacency Start with the Same Four Letters

Counterproductive sales compensation plans create a lot of problems that could be solved easily if the cause was recognized. What's curious is why executives frustrated by these sales problems often refuse to look at the comp plans they've created as the genesis of the issue.

It is commonplace for an executive who's considering engaging me to rattle off a litany of complaints he has with his sales organization: They're lazy. Complacent. Loaded down in administrative details. Refuse to prospect. Too involved in operations. Pander to their pet accounts. Obsessed with renewals. And so on. This list is very familiar to me.

He'll then point the finger at all kinds of potential causes—Gen Y, lack of sales skills, bad parenting, poor sales leadership, the economy, the U.S. Congress—but almost never at his comp plan.

After letting the executive vent, I'll ask a variety of questions about his people, culture, expectations, goals, sales manager, etc. And I usually save this one for last: "Tell me about your sales compensation plan and whether it's driving the behaviors you designed it to." It's pretty darn rare to get a coherent answer to that question. I typically hear excuses, apologies, or some rationale for why his plan makes sense even though it's not working. Sometimes, an executive will pause or mumble something unintelligible and then admit that maybe his plan isn't accomplishing what it's supposed to and that he would like help looking at it.

Salespeople Pay Very Close Attention to How They Are Compensated

A couple years ago, I was preparing a presentation on sales management for a Vistage CEO group's monthly meeting. One of my clients invited me to attend because several members were facing sales leadership challenges. As is typical for me, I got emotional while drafting the material. In this case, I was exasperated from working with a particular client led by a high-ego, sales know-it-all CEO. When he would talk about compensation, he repeatedly used an expression that made my skin crawl: "I'm willing to pay them XYZ." This CEO spoke about sales compensation as if he was writing a personal check to the salesperson. As hard as I tried, and believe me I tried, I could not get the point across to this man that he wasn't *paying* them. Under an appropriate compensation plan, the salesperson *earns* his pay.

This particular company's plan was beyond convoluted. Worse, it was based on total territory sales with very little tied to new business development. Several members of the sales team complained to me that regardless of the success they achieved closing new business, their large territories and the formula used to calculate compensation prevented them from moving the needle enough to affect their pay. In essence, the comp plan design served as a disincentive to hunt for new business because new deals couldn't move total territory revenue enough to trigger meaningful commission. You need neither a consulting background nor a crystal ball to accurately predict how that situation unfolded. Very simply, the salespeople lost their intensity to hunt for new clients because it didn't pay.

Here's the reality: Salespeople work the compensation plan. And the best salespeople are the best at working the comp plan. That's not news to anyone. But knowing the truth and acting on it are two different things, which brings me back to preparing that presentation for the Vistage group. While mentally rehashing my frustration with the CEO and client company described previously, I typed the words *compensation* and *complacency* into a PowerPoint slide. As I stared at the screen, it hit me. Compensation and complacency begin with the same four letters. Voila! For a brief moment I saw myself as Isaac Newton or Thomas Edison celebrating some grandiose discovery. Granted, I doubt I'm the first human to make that observation, but since I haven't read it anywhere else, and the Google search comes up clean except for a blog post written by yours truly, I'm putting my name on it. No, it's not the Theory of Relativity or the lightbulb, but it sure is true in sales. If you have COMPlacent salespeople, start your analysis by looking at the COMPensation plan.

Flat Compensation Plans Send a Horrible Message

One of the most common and most dangerous problems with sales compensation plans is that they are too *flat*. By *flat*, I mean that there is nowhere near enough of a difference between what the very top and the very bottom performers earn. These communistic, paternalistic, politically correct compensation plans make sense only to the non-sales, non-performance-driven, egalitarian leaders who write them. When the spread between what the best and the worst salespeople in an organization earn is too small, there are serious consequences that actually accomplish the exact opposite of what a smart comp plan should do.

Under a flat plan, where the annual compensation earned by members of the sales force is tightly clustered around the median, salespeople who are not carrying their weight end up overpaid at the expense of severely underpaying the top producers. Think about how silly that is. Those who aren't cutting it are overcompensated for what they produce, while those bringing in the lion's share of the business are essentially cheated. What results from this silliness? Those on the bottom of the sales ranking, who we'd want to be uncomfortable, dissatisfied with their take-home pay, and hungry, end up actually being quite comfortable. Why would they change their intensity level or behavior if they're handsomely rewarded for underachieving? Instead of these employees being forced to either improve or look for work elsewhere, flat plans provide them a nice safety net and incentive to stay. Ugh!

On the flip side, consider the message sent to the driven, overachieving, super-committed top producer. She sees the tiny delta between what she's earning and what underperformers are getting paid and starts asking herself hard questions: How is this fair? Why am I killing myself to produce for this company and have so little to show for it? Do these people even appreciate me? Eventually she ramps up her self-talk to another level altogether: Hmmm, she thinks, I wonder what other companies in this space would pay a top producer? Why should I stay here if I barely make more than these jokers who sell half as much as I do?

It bears repeating: A flat compensation plan accomplishes the opposite of what a smart plan should. It provides underperformers comfort to stick around while simultaneously discouraging the overachievers, causing them to either back off or to shop their talents and achievements elsewhere.

All Sales Dollars Are Not the Same!

A dollar is not a dollar, at least when it comes to sales compensation. So many executives and financial people take an overly simple macro view of sales commission. On financial statements and in bank accounts all dollars are equal, but the same is not true when paying salespeople. All *sales dollars* are not equal, not even close.

Which is more important for successful revenue growth: a dollar of sales to an existing customer that is simply continuing to purchase what it always has, or an incremental dollar of sales because that customer purchases something new? Similarly, which is a better indicator of successful proactive selling: a dollar of sales to a current client or a dollar of sales to a newly acquired client?

I understand that maintaining existing business is often an important piece of the sales function, and that *losing* existing business creates a deficit that needs to be made up before growing incrementally. I'm not arguing that fact. But from a revenue growth perspective, which I believe is the primary objective of a sales organization—to grow the top line, not just maintain it—capturing a *new dollar* of sales is way more valuable than recapturing an existing dollar of sales. Can we agree that if revenue growth is the primary goal of the sales team, then a new dollar sold is not only more important, but also a better measure of sales effectiveness and worthy of higher compensation? And if we can agree on that, doesn't it make infinitely more sense not to commission all sales dollars the same, but instead to pay more commission for a new sale and less for an existing sale?

Paying higher commission rates for new sales and lower rates for repeat sales is a simple concept. But the reason I devoted so much space prefacing my argument is because even when executives agree conceptually, many have a difficult time pulling the trigger on that type of compensation change. Time and time again, I see sales organizations struggling to bring in new business where one of the main culprits is a compensation plan that does not handsomely reward sellers for acquiring new pieces of business. Think about it. Why would a salesperson who is fat, dumb, and happy, managing a healthy portfolio or book of business, and very much enjoying the living that portfolio throws off, not over-service those existing accounts? It's not any more complex than that. If you get paid the same for babysitting current customers as you would for doing the heavy lifting to acquire new ones, where would you spend your time? Furthermore, why would you even risk taking your eye off the ball and maintaining your current base of business when there is no penalty for playing a *prevent defense* and no incentive to go on the sales offensive?

Commission Annuities Create Cruise Control Sellers

Sales commission is useful as a tool to drive behavior only if it is variable. There are two critical premises underlying effective commission. One, commission has to be *earned*, meaning that you have to do something to get it. And two, as just stated, commission must be variable, meaning that the amount earned changes based on actual results. Commission that comes automatically every month (or quarter, or whatever period your company uses) and feels like an annuity payment to the salesperson really isn't commission. Oh, it's called commission on a pay stub and on the profit and loss statement. But let's not kid ourselves. When this *variable* component of compensation is not variable at all but shows up like clockwork whether or not you sell anything new or even bother to get out of bed, it is commission in name only. The reality is that it's a giant gift and might as well be considered additional base salary.

I worked with two companies not long ago that deployed a straightforward territory manager model. At first glance I was really encouraged to see that their compensation plans were not flat at all. Their top territory managers, who were truly gifted salespeople, way out-earned the average sales team member. Both client companies were facing a similar challenge of trying to get their top dog territory managers to prospect for new business. In one of the companies, the number one guy was given an expanded territory ripe with prospective customers. Everyone, including the territory manager, agreed it was a great growth opportunity. In the other company, the top producer was charged with pursuing a named list of highly strategic target prospects in geographically attractive and easy-to-get-to locations. He agreed that it made sense to pursue these prospects, and he was comfortable going after the business.

Both initiatives failed miserably. Neither salesperson put in the required effort to proactively pursue the agreed-to target prospects. What prevented these perfectly qualified star sellers from going on the attack? One big reason we've already covered. The territory managers in both (unrelated) companies already had plenty on their respective plates and were taking home significant dollars. One of the guys was making close to $300K managing his large territory and some major customers. So the fact that this new initiative to prospect didn't come with special incentive in the form of increased commission rates helped doom it from the start. After the fact, the territory manager practically admitted that he felt compelled to over-serve his large customers and couldn't rationalize the risk of diverting his attention from these accounts.

Even more interesting, however, is what we learned from the other territory manager. It turns out that this high producer, unbeknownst to senior management, had been operating on cruise control for quite some time. Sure, he was referred to as the "number one guy," but the truth is that he was really just caretaking the number one territory. The "commission" base was solid because he'd been around forever, serving this very loyal group of customers. His company was so entrenched at these accounts that the commissions were going to come whether he worked the territory or not. The "not" turned out to be the case. And this focused initiative helped all of us to uncover that it wasn't just that he wasn't prospecting—he wasn't working his existing customers either!

Commission works only when it's truly variable and requires work to earn it! Compensation and complacency are more intertwined than is often acknowledged.

CHAPTER 11

An Anti-Sales Culture Disengages the Heart of the Sales Team

There is an interesting phenomenon that contributes to anti-sales cultures in many organizations. People tend to be more jealous or unappreciative of those in sales than in any other role in a business. Non-salespeople, be they C-Suite executives, members of the finance department, or production line workers, can be disposed to believe that sales is easy, that sales is glamorous, that salespeople make too much money for what they do. What's so intriguing about these popular opinions is that when the stone throwers are offered the opportunity to try their own hand at sales, they are quick to decline. They may love to critique and poke fun at sellers, boldly declaring how easy and wonderful it must be to be in sales, but deep down they know they couldn't do it themselves. And the voices, attitudes, and policies emanating from these jealous critics often do significant damage to the heart-engagement and performance of sales organizations.

A Miserable Accountant Can Still Do Great Work; the Same Is Not True for a Miserable Salesperson

Sales is a unique type of job. To do it successfully, you have to want to sell. Think about that statement for a minute. A salesperson has to *want to sell*. There is no way to effectively prospect for new business or penetrate a challenging existing customer if your heart is not in it. A miserable salesperson cannot represent her company, her solution, or herself well. If her heart is not engaged, she won't fight to get in. She won't be able to woo a prospect. She won't go the extra step to ask the hard questions, push past initial resistance, fight back hard against objections, or continue to pursue deals that seem to have gone dark.

This may come off as harsh, or even biased, but it's true: a miserable accountant can still do great work. An accountant doesn't require passion to close the books at month-end. An accountant can literally hate her job and yet produce accurate, timely, and valuable financial statements. But good luck trying to find a miserable salesperson who is bringing in new business and delivering her numbers month in and month out. You'll be looking for a long time because she doesn't exist. Miserable, mistreated salespeople don't sell. There are no miserable top performers in sales. Why? Because when their company's anti-sales culture gets out of control, top producers go elsewhere.

Arbitrary Commission Deductions and Compensation Adjustments Result in Miserable Sales Teams

The ironic twist to this discussion about how heart-engagement affects different types of employees differently is that it's often an out-of-control accountant (or accounting department) creating misery for the sales team. Now, I won't go as far as declaring that misery loves company and that there are people in finance departments intentionally trying to get the goat of salespeople, but it sure seems that's the case in a lot of companies!

Nothing will suck the life, energy, and trust out of a sales team faster than an over-empowered accountant making arbitrary commission deductions. I've seen this time and time again and it is infuriating. The controller at the last company where I worked was notorious for this. My sales team already had plenty of issues with this woman because there was zero confidence in the way the company costed out jobs at a time when there was an initiative to switch from revenue-based commission to a gross margin–based commission. It was bad enough that we didn't trust her numbers, but the animosity and mistrust skyrocketed when she began to regularly make one-sided adjustments to monthly commission statements. Every month there would be a complaint line outside my door on the day commission statements were issued.

Listen, all of us in sales understood that the controller was trying to do her job and protect the company financially. That wasn't the issue. The issue was that she'd take these deductions without asking enough questions or involving the salespeople affected. As a result, her actions came across as both arbitrary and heavy-handed. I'm not sure how you react when someone takes money away from you that you believe with 100 percent certainty you earned, but I know how cheated, angry, and exasperated that makes me feel.

A larger consequence of the controller's actions was that the company's senior executives and owners turned a blind eye to the situation. The complaining was loud enough each month that they knew it was happening. But the fact that leadership allowed it to continue spoke volumes to the sales team and to me about how little it valued the sales organization. Unfortunately, this is not an isolated example. I see this type of executive-endorsed mistreatment of sales teams in a variety of businesses. I also see the corresponding reduction in passion and effort by the sales force in response to it.

There Are Consequences for Not Appreciating and Acknowledging the Sales Effort

In companies with *healthy* attitudes toward sales, salespeople and sales victories are celebrated. Sure, there are always the few detractors or those who snicker when a salesperson gets recognized. That comes with the territory. But in these healthy situations, there is at least a general understanding of an important fact: The livelihood of everyone else in the organization is dependent on the sales force doing its job and doing it well. It makes good business sense to recognize and thank the sales team for a job well done.

A lack of appreciation for the sales team manifests itself in various ways—sometimes rather subtly, and sometimes more overtly. One of the most blatant examples I've experienced transpired a few years ago following a client's record sales quarter. During the company's quarterly meeting/conference call, which included the sales leader, the sales team, and employees from every department, the outspokenly anti-sales CEO reported the record revenue numbers with much fanfare. He then made a point to specifically and publicly thank just about every department for their outstanding effort. Big props and praise were directed to engineering, production, finance, and several key leaders in the company. Which department wasn't mentioned following a record *sales* quarter? You guessed it. Sales. And do you know how I know this even though I wasn't present for the meeting? Three members of the sales team either called or text messaged me afterward to express their disappointment and anger toward the CEO and the company.

At this company, the anti-sales culture went way beyond a lack of appreciation; *acrimony* might be the best word to describe the executive committee's feelings toward the sales organization. It was so bad that I found myself wondering if I could even continue the engagement. I was personally offended by this disrespectful attitude, and I didn't even work there! Taking one last shot to get my point across, I put my observations in writing, hoping to communicate to these executives how deeply serious their problem was. Here is an excerpt from that memo:

> *(Company Name redacted) has a significant anti-sales culture, one of the worst I've seen. (CEO Name redacted) is the major driver of this, and I will address it in more detail with him personally. The lack of respect for the sales team as a whole is obvious; it is damaging, and it is communicated in some not-so-subtle ways. The fact that (Company Name redacted) just completed its best quarter ever in terms of revenue and profit, yet during the company meeting and conference call, (CEO Name redacted) neither gave credit to the sales team nor thanked the team or individual members speaks volumes. (CEO Name redacted) is communicating his displeasure with the sales team in a very clear manner and the sales team hears him. . . .*
>
> *Sales is as much about the heart as it is about the head. We have talked about this extensively, but it is not sinking in at (Company Name redacted). While I have been around many organizations with anti-sales cultures where salespeople are belittled, micro-managed, or even abused, your company is the first I've seen categorically deny credit to individual salespeople for successes to this extent. You may feel that the salespeople do not deserve credit for the results at certain accounts. And you may even be partially correct in some cases, but there is no way to have a healthy, energized, fully engaged sales team when the norm is to blame salespeople for issues (i.e., slow pricing turnaround, etc.), yet completely deflect credit to others in the company for sales successes.*

You can identify a company with an anti-sales undercurrent pretty easily. Not only is the sales force routinely not recognized for what it achieves, but in these companies it is also fashionable to openly complain and criticize those in sales with a broad brush. In *New Sales. Sim-*

plified. I offered a sampling of things I hear when it's open season to pick on sales. This sampling bears repeating here:

"The salespeople use too many samples." "The sales team isn't using the materials we gave them." "The sales team is authorizing too many returns." "Your people are not attending the all-company meeting on Tuesdays." "How come he took that million-dollar client to such an expensive dinner?" "Have the salespeople do their paperwork and admin on weekends." "Did you see the proposal we sent out? It was awful." "The plant really screwed up this big order; grab a few salespeople to help unpack and repack these boxes; they're not doing anything anyway." "Why did he fly to Nashville when it's only a five-hour drive?" "Tell the salespeople they can ship out their own sample requests." "She tipped 18 percent, and our policy clearly states that we should only tip 15 percent." "That customer is complaining that the salesperson didn't return his call within 38 seconds." And so on.

Important people in your organization may think it's cute or fun to pick on the sales team. Jealous non-salespeople appear to get pleasure from doing it. But nothing good results, and when it goes too far or happens too often, your top sales producers are going to walk. As mentioned earlier, there are no out-of-work top salespeople because there is such a shortage of excellent sales talent. So, if you foster an environment that under-appreciates sales, understand that you'll very likely lose those A-players on your team that you most want to keep, and disengage the hearts of those who stay.

CHAPTER 12

The Big Ego Senior Executive "Sales Expert" Often Does More Harm than Good

If I'm being completely transparent, I must admit that this is a difficult chapter to write. But the book's subtitle promises the "Straight Truth," and what's included here needs to be shared—for the benefit of both those who *will be* offended and the sales teams they lead.

I have the names of nine CEOs listed in my notes pertaining to this chapter. Their names, voices, and faces will be etched forever in my mind. While I learned much and benefited greatly from my time with each of these men (yes, all nine of these particular CEOs happen to be of the male persuasion), collectively, they provided numerous powerful examples and painful lessons of how high-ego senior executives who consider themselves "sales experts" can do tremendous damage to their own company's sales efforts.

All but one of the chief executives were leading companies between $15 million and $200 million in annual revenue when I either worked for or consulted for them. The other company was significantly larger. Most of these the chief executives also happen to be the founders of their companies.

An Embarrassing Sales Call Can Derail a Sales Effort

Writing this, I am imagining the smiles, chuckles, and shaking heads as thousands of salespeople begin to relive nightmare sales calls made alongside a *sales expert* senior executive. Before I go further, let me make one thing abundantly clear: I am a huge proponent of executive selling and team selling. The right senior executive in front of the right customer playing the right role at the right time can be a thing of sales beauty and produce a highly desirable outcome. Unfortunately, the wrong high-ego senior executive saying the wrong thing at the wrong time often creates a painful, embarrassing situation that derails the sales effort instead of supporting it.

I have observed CEOs who boldly preach the importance of proper sales call structure and asking great probing questions spend 90 percent of a sales call talking. And what do they spend so much time talking about? Themselves. Their accomplishments. The companies they have built. Their own brilliance, methods, business theories, and, of course, the solution they've come to sell. I've also watched senior executives self-destruct because they misread a prospect's political leaning and incorrectly felt safe making extreme political statements. And in possibly the most bizarre sales call of my career, I cringed as my CEO blabbered incoherent nonsense for an entire hour while sitting across the table from a C-Suite executive at a giant dream prospect. At the conclusion of the meeting, the prospect looked right at my CEO with a dead-serious face and asked, "Now tell me one more time, exactly what is it that your company does?" Shoot me now, I thought. What made this last example so humorous (and painful) is that this particular CEO personally *wrote* our company's "story" and was convinced he was the only who could truly tell it the way it needed to be told.

Constant Pontificating and Micromanaging Deflates the Sales Team

It's not just in front of customers and prospects that our high-ego senior execs can't seem to control themselves. Their boorish behavior in sales team meetings or when playing surrogate sales manager can take the air out of salespeople's sails in a nanosecond.

I remember the time I spent an entire day building up a downtrodden sales team but mistakenly asked the CEO to briefly wrap up the afternoon with a few comments to the troops before heading out for our team celebration dinner. Did I mention that *I was the one* who thought it was a good idea to have the big boss close out the day before dinner? The CEO spent almost an hour pontificating on his own sales theories, then berating sales team members for living in the past and making excuses for why their results weren't better. I leaned against the wall of the conference room watching whatever goodwill had been built that day go up in smoke. The body language of the sales team spoke volumes as they slumped in their chairs, many with arms crossed and blank stares. Even if the CEO had some valid points (which he certainly did), his approach was wrong and unhelpful. As you can imagine, our "celebration dinner" didn't have much of a celebratory feel to it.

Please don't think that these senior executives saved up their most deflating behavior for special occasions like the example above. Oh, no. The *Divine Nine* chief executives from my list found opportunities to preach their deep sales expertise on a regular basis. If there was an open pulpit, they'd find it. One of these CEOs liked to lead both the weekly sales team meeting and the weekly executive committee meeting. The best part of that? Both meetings typically occurred the same day! What a treat, as I got observe this man dominate not one, but two meetings.

It was Monday madness for sure. Every week I'd come to work fully charged, self-motivated, and ready to take on the world and win.

By the time we exited the Monday morning weekly sales team meeting (which was slated for an hour but would often go two), the positive energy I started the day with was gone. Gone, gone. The CEO would alternate between interrogating individual salespeople about how they were handling specific opportunities and grabbing a dry-erase marker so he could diagram out his sales theories on the whiteboard. He wanted to ensure that his fingerprints were all over this sales team, and he succeeded. One hundred percent of the time we walked out of that sales team meeting exasperated and exhausted. Great way to start the sales week, don't you think?

Another one of these founder/CEOs had great pride in his technical knowledge. He not only took pleasure in sharing this extensive knowledge with members of his sales team at odd times, he'd go a step further and regularly quiz the salespeople about certain formulas that he deemed important. The problem with his habit was not that he wanted the salespeople to be technically competent. There's certainly nothing ill-advised about that. It was that he would use these opportunities to embarrass individuals. The CEO would intentionally ask these questions publicly, knowing there was a high likelihood that the answers would be incorrect. It may seem like a small thing, but it had a significant negative affect on members of the sales team, who regularly mentioned that it bothered them.

There is another intriguing commonality among several of the men on my list: They were often more concerned with a salesperson's activity level than her results. Just let that preference and the implications sink in for a minute.

There's a word for it when the big boss cares more about how you spend your time than he does about what you produce, and it's an ugly word: Micromanagement.

Working for a control-freak micromanager is unpleasant enough, but when you add that characteristic to our already unflattering list, it's typically the final straw:

Embarrassing + Pontificating + Micromanaging = Disengaged Team

This obsession with activity plays itself out in bizarre ways. I have recently had hard conversations with two chief executives (both founders, self-proclaimed sales gurus, and very close to retirement age). Each of these men absolutely insists on receiving call reports from members of the sales team. Both want to know whom their people are calling, how often, what took place during the meeting, etc. On the surface, it sounds innocent. Their insistence on personally reviewing these reports is always carefully couched within a broader sales issue. Sometimes they'll talk about the importance of a high-frequency sales effort, which I'm a huge fan of, or the need to monitor the percent of sales calls that turn into new opportunities. Listen, I'm all about key activity metrics and proclaiming that a high-frequency sales attack almost always beats a low-frequency attack. That's not the problem.

My issue is not whether we should be asking the sales team for call reports and monitoring activity levels; it's with *who* is asking for this information. At a recent lunch meeting, I was with one of these CEOs who was doing his best to explain how important it was for him to know every client and prospective client his national sales team of ten was calling on. He wasn't hearing me as I tried to convey that he was both usurping the authority of several layers of management below him and simultaneously sending the wrong message to the sales team. In frustration, I grabbed a pen and drew out the layers of his very hierarchical company. "CEO Name, there's you, and below you we have the COO/GM who is over the vice president of sales. And under him we have a national sales manager who is over the sales force. You are four layers removed from the people in the field. What does it say to the sales team that you need to see their call reports and personally monitor their activity? To me, it says that you are a control freak. It also broadcasts loud and clear that you trust neither the people you have in management nor the salespeople. It's hurting the sales effort, undermining your sales leaders, and causing the salespeople to ask questions we'd prefer they not ask. That's why I strongly encourage you to review reports about actual results and to monitor the health of the corporate sales pipeline. But please stop asking for daily activity and call reports!" Conversations like these are a good reminder to me why consultants should always get paid upfront. Sure, I write that tongue-in-cheek, but I am not kidding. It's much easier to tell the person who hired you the hard truth he supposedly wants to hear after his check clears the bank.

Let me clarify: Senior executive involvement in the sales effort can be a very positive influence. When a founder or CEO engages appropriately as a mentor to managers and salespeople, or participates on sales calls to make customers feel special and appreciated, that is very powerful. But, as described in this chapter, ego and a strong desire to control often get in the way and cause a well-meaning CEO to do more harm than good.

CHAPTER 13

Entrepreneurial, Visionary Leaders Forget That Their People Can't Do What They Can Do

In the previous chapter we looked at how (negative/less than flattering) traits of the senior leader can damage the sales team. Let's shift gears and examine how, surprisingly, sometimes the greatest strengths of the entrepreneurial, charismatic executive can actually impede a sales team's success.

Your People Are Not You

One of the reasons I absolutely love what I do to earn a living is because I get the opportunity to work with some incredibly gifted people. My notes for this chapter include a list of ten super-talented, visionary business leaders. These senior executives have produced some of my most fun projects and client relationships because they often have boundless positive energy and are continually a step or more ahead of their team and me. These idea machines dazzle us with their ability to create and improvise on the fly, to sell concepts that don't yet exist, and to paint exquisite pictures of a brighter future to any audience. That's the *good side* of working for such a talented charismatic leader. However, there is a *downside* that is much more difficult to discern. Only after observing the same problem in multiple organizations was I finally able to recognize and begin calling it out to help clients identify and overcome the issue.

Several years ago, I was sitting with an extremely driven, extroverted, and charismatic CEO at the big glass conference table he used as a desk. It was our first meeting. I was entertained, amused, and even a bit shocked at his level of intensity and charm. His personality filled the room—in a good way. I loved everything about this guy, including his cool shoes. And as he explained his vision for the company and the various major initiatives he was undertaking, I began to get a sense for the monumental task he was asking of his salespeople. The specific details aren't important to the story. What's key to my point is how many moving pieces there were, and that this hugely talented sales chief was asking the sales team to sell a solution that was still on the drawing board to people and prospects who were unfamiliar and didn't yet understand how to buy this type of new offering. Said differently, he was asking people who had never sold this type of solution to sell something that didn't truly yet exist to clients who weren't quite ready, even though they would likely be looking for this type of solution in the future. Got it?

One of the reasons I was sitting across the big glass table from this man was because of his growing frustration that the sales team wasn't getting it done. In three different ways he told me that he couldn't comprehend what was so hard about what he was asking his salespeople to do. With each example he'd tell me the story of a major sales success from his own career and how *he* was able to sell giant, transformational deals with essentially smoke and mirrors. At that instant, the penny dropped and it all came together in my mind. I raised my eyebrows and began to smirk. In his loud, playful voice he shouted not to hold out on him. "What? Tell me!" he insisted. "[CEO Name], don't you see what's happening?" I responded. "They're not you! They can't do what you can do. You get away with it because of the force of your personality, your outrageous, probably dangerous level of confidence, and your sick ability to sell a vision."

He let out an audible "hmm," sat back in his chair, put two fingers up to his lips, and sat there pondering my assessment. Frankly, I found it hard to believe this was news to him. He knew how supremely talented he was and had the swagger to prove it. Yet for some reason, he just assumed that because he could do it, his salespeople should be able to as well. What's even more surprising is how many times I've seen similar situations in other organizations run by supremely gifted, charismatic entrepreneurs.

The Absence of Clarity Dooms the Sales Attack

After this ridiculously talented sales superstar CEO digested my observation that his team required just a wee bit more support and a significantly more concrete plan of attack than he did, I asked a few more pointed questions about the clarity of his strategy, and he wrapped up the meeting by asking me to come back in a week.

I was back at the glass table a week later as my charismatic new friend (and now client) started the meeting by saying that I caused him to lose sleep. I usually help my clients sleep better knowing that we are going to systematically address their sales issues, so his statement took me aback. He went on to share that one thing I said really upset his apple cart, and he couldn't get it out of his head. During our first meeting, I was recapping my frustration at another client and with my most recent employer. Each company was operating in a highly entrepreneurial mode with strategies that were in flux and about as clear as mud. This lack of clarity created havoc for the sales team. The little phrase I used that bothered the CEO was my declaration that "sales follows strategy."

That's where we picked up the conversation and I expanded on my premise that clarity from the top was a nonnegotiable prerequisite for a successful new business development sales attack. The job of the sales force is to execute the company's strategy to perfection, not to create it on the fly. Clarity is absolutely essential when asking salespeople to execute a proactive new business sales attack. I have yet to see an individual salesperson or a sales team succeed in the marketplace without a crystal-clear picture of the mission. Salespeople can't be making up their strategy as they go. It's the job of senior company leadership to clearly point the sales force in the right direction:

- ► Which markets should they be pursuing and why?

- ► Exactly what are we asking the sales force to sell and, specifically, to whom should they be selling it?

You may chuckle thinking that these are obvious or ridiculous questions, but I assure you they are not. I've been in enough companies in a state of transition where senior management couldn't clearly articulate these answers. Yet what is intriguing, and frankly infuriating, is that these very executives are quick to blame the sales team when business doesn't come in at the desired rate. Excuse me, but when did a business's strategy fall to the sales force? I must have missed that day in business school.

Often, what's portrayed as a "sales problem" isn't a sales problem at all. The company and its senior leaders have a responsibility to provide the sales organization with strategic direction. As I've written before, "Mr. CEO, please do your job so we can do ours." That request is not intended with any disrespect. It's simply a plea for help (and direction) so we can succeed. In early meetings with my own prospective clients, I make it a habit to ask about the company's strategy and the demand for its offerings in targeted markets. I try to make it abundantly clear: I don't do strategy and neither should your sales team. If you can't clearly tell us where to pursue new business and don't have evidence that there is demand for what you sell, then it's a strategy problem, not necessarily a "sales problem." Sure, many entrepreneurs and visionaries tend to be comfortable in those free-flowing, entrepreneurial environments where they are forced to build their strategy on the fly. They love operating in those conditions. But that doesn't translate into success for the sales team. Time and time again I've seen salespeople flounder and fail without clear direction from the top.

CHAPTER 14

The Lack of Coaching and Mentoring Produces Ineffective Salespeople

Back in the day, sales managers were responsible for developing the sales skills of their people. Most managers took great pride in mentoring those under their care to greatness. Today, not so much.

Managers Are Working Less in the Field and Not Developing Their People

Coaching salespeople, particularly on basic selling skills, has fallen by the wayside. Sales managers seem to be more consumed with pleasing the executive committee, plowing through their huge administrative burden, and managing the team via the CRM and email (as discussed in Chapter 4). Managers are spending less and less time in the field with outside sellers, or alongside members of the inside sales team. It's as if the "ride-along" is now a lost art. And sales team meetings are rarely used for sales skills training anymore. When training is on the agenda for a sales meeting, the majority of the time is spent on product training, not sales skill training.

The resulting reduction in sales effectiveness is having devastating effects on many sales organizations. Most salespeople have not had good consultative selling modeled for them, or benefited from having a seasoned seller along on sales calls.

I have great memories and stories of being mentored as a young sales pup. In fact, I am *still* using many of the skills and techniques shown me by sales managers and executives who personally invested in my development. Much of that mentoring happened out in the field, where they'd join me on trips to see customers and prospects. They'd coach and prepare me before sales calls, and following the meeting we would discuss what went well and where I could improve. In addition, having the sales manager or head of sales out in the field was an opportunity to expose them firsthand to the reality of what I was facing in the marketplace! It's one thing to *tell* management why you're struggling to grow the business in certain markets. It's another all together when you can *show* them in person.

Sales leaders early in my career helped mold me into a professional. Twenty-five years ago my first manager taught me how to prepare for a trip: where to get a shoe shine, how to pack, how to use plastic dry cleaner bags to keep clothes from wrinkling, and why you should always, always, always bring an extra dress shirt along for those mornings you discover a stain or a missing button. Just this month I was in a hotel room getting dressed for a keynote talk I'd be delivering to 400 people. As I went to get the shirt off the hanger, the neck button crumbled in my fingers. Without skipping a beat, I reached for my spare shirt, chuckled, and said aloud, "Thank you, Bob Smith."

Bob was a classic old-school sales manager. Dark suit. Shiny shoes. Slicked-back hair. Slightly overzealous. His picture should be in the dictionary next to the word *indefatigable*. He taught me a ton about sales but also had some weird habits that created vivid memories. One of my favorites was having to take him to Hardee's late at night near the Holiday Inn in Springdale, Arkansas. This is where we'd stay when calling on Walmart headquarters. On every single trip to see Walmart, Bob would make me go to the Hardee's drive-thru the night before so he could bring two large black coffees back to the hotel with him. To be honest, I am not even sure the guy ever slept. But he sure was ready to rumble when they'd put us in those tiny buyer meeting rooms just past the lobby inside Walmart's office.

Salespeople Are Not Raising Their Game as Fast as Buyers

Across the board, sales skills are degrading, not improving. Recently, two client executives from completely different industries shared the same fear with me. Both lamented the fact that buyers were learning, growing, and adapting faster than sellers. Buyers were better trained and possessed better business acumen and skills than those attempting to sell to them. I agree, and believe that if the current trajectory is not altered there is big trouble ahead for the sales profession.

We'll take a deeper look at best practices for sales managers working in the field in Chapter 22. But for now, I would like to challenge you with this question: If you're not teaching selling skills in sales team meetings, and the sales manager is not out of the office and working in the field rotating through members of the sales team, then who *is* helping your salespeople become more proficient? Who is developing their skills? And how would you even begin to know how your salespeople come across in front of a customer?

In many industries, selling has never been harder. The Internet, which can be a powerful sales tool, also works against salespeople by empowering buyers with more information than once thought possible. Potential customers have reams of data available at the click of a mouse. Salespeople used to be a great source of information for buyers. Customers *needed* salespeople. That fact alone made it easy to get appointments.

Today, that is not the case. Buyers gather and process copious amounts of information long before a salesperson ever gets there. To compound the issue, prospective customers are busier than ever. They are being asked to do more with less. Time is at a premium. The last thing a buyer wants is to take a meeting with a salesperson who only supplies information but doesn't create value during the interaction.

The bar is being raised in terms of what is expected of professional sellers. The brilliant Neil Rackham, author of *SPIN Selling* (New York: McGraw-Hill, 1988), and possibly one of the greatest sales minds of this generation, offers a powerful question in a video promoting Matthew Dixon and Brent Adamson's book *The Challenger Sale* (New York: Portfolio/Penguin, 2011), Rackham suggests that to determine if salespeople are doing a "good job" in front of the customer, we should ask this question:

> *"Are your people making the kind of sales calls where the customer would write a check for the sales call . . . because the sales call did something so useful for the customer that the customer values it?"*

Sure, that's a very high standard, but what a great question and powerful challenge from Rackham. Based on my own observations, in just about every case, the answer to that question is no. The majority of salespeople are not conducting that kind of sales call or being perceived by customers as creating that level of value.

In the next chapter I unpack several common reasons salespeople are being perceived as nothing more than vendors/suppliers/product pushers and not the value-creating, consultative sales professionals we so badly want them to be.

CHAPTER 15

Amateurish Salespeople Are Perceived Simply as Vendors, Pitchmen, and Commodity Sellers

Sales leaders and businesses are paying a hefty price for not developing the selling skills of their people. They're not only selling less than they could be, they're also being forced to sell at lower prices than they should be!

Sure, some of this is caused by better trained buyers armed with better information. Many large organizations now employ professional procurement departments that specialize in a unique form of torture: putting the salesperson in a figurative vise and tightening the grip until all the life and margin are squeezed out of him and the deal. Commoditization is ugly indeed, and being treated as nothing more than a "vendor" is insulting and de-motivating to any professional seller.

The real problem, however, is not the more sophisticated customer and its procurement processes; it's that there are so few in sales who are truly *professional sellers*. It's salespeople's own approach, attitude, and behavior that is shooting their sales effort in the foot while causing buyers to perceive them as nothing more than vendors and commodity sellers rather than the professional problem solvers and value creators we so badly want them to be.

Salespeople Living in Reactive Mode Are Arriving Late to Opportunities

Probably the most common and damaging driver of salespeople being perceived and treated simply as vendors is being late to a sales opportunity. Sales leaders allow their teams to spend way too much time operating in *reactive mode*. Sellers are waiting for leads, waiting for customers to raise their hands, waiting for beautifully teed-up opportunities. Waiting, waiting, waiting.

There are a plethora of reasons salespeople are so often last to a deal and late to the party. For one, many of today's prevailing sales theorists mistakenly promote the notion that proactive prospecting is dead. These new "experts" tell us that it's fruitless to pursue a prospect that isn't coming to you. They quote crazy statistics, telling everyone that today's modern buyer is 70 percent through the buying process before engaging a salesperson. "Don't call them; they'll call you when they're ready" is what these experts declare.

I take issue with the many loud voices preaching these deadly lies. These theories are not only wrong, they're dangerous. They're particularly dangerous because today's under-mentored and under-coached salespeople are gullible. The sole reason prospects get that far along in their buying journey without having engaged with a salesperson is that reactive salespeople are sitting on their butts waiting for the prospect to raise their hand and call them in! The oft-quoted statistic above is a bogus straw man propagated by supposed experts with an agenda. This nonsense that sellers shouldn't be pursuing prospective clients is exactly what lazy, reactive salespeople want to hear, and it's killing them.

Whether it's from listening to bad advice or simply from practicing bad work habits, the end result is the same. Reactive sellers are often slow arriving to a new sales opportunity. By the time they're involved, the buyer is far down the path. Buying criteria have been established. Even worse, these reactive sellers end up way at the back of the line. Often, they find themselves playing catch-up to their more proactive competitors' salespeople, who got there first, who were building relationships before the buyer started shopping, who were in what I call "Position A": sitting in the consultant's seat, bringing value, sharing insights, and helping define the buyer's requirements.

Can you see why being late to the opportunity often relegates your salesperson to vendor status? How hard is it to be seen as a value creator and consultant to the prospective customer who is already far down the path? Very hard. It's no fun selling from behind, eating the dust of your competitor who already has a relationship and earned a seat at the table because he was in the opportunity early. In fact, it might very well be that your competitor actually *created* the opportunity by proactively targeting the customer. Unless your solution is so radically different from and superior to the competition's, which I hate to tell you is rarely the case, it is very hard to come across as a consultative, value-creating salesperson when you're tardy. Typically, from that position, it takes a very low price to earn the buyer's attention. And that's a game we certainly don't want to play.

Salespeople Who Lead with Their Product Are Asking to Be Commoditized

Adding insult to injury, after they're slow to get involved in a potential sales opportunity, many salespeople further reduce their effectiveness by leading with their product or solution. Again, it's untrained or poorly trained sellers who don't know any better. They put their product out front and make it the focus of the conversation when meeting with potential customers. What are the consequences of making the offering the hero of the story? That approach communicates—loud and clear—to the customer that the salesperson is self-focused, more concerned with what he's selling than with the customer's issues, needs, and desires. Think about it. It's a truly horrible message to send.

When salespeople lead with their product or service, it is impossible to be perceived as consultants or trusted advisors. It makes it as clear as day that the salesperson believes the relationship and sale are centered on his offering, not the customer and its needs. It's as if the salesperson is begging the customer to put his offering's features and price on a spreadsheet to be compared against every competitors' features and price. The salesperson might as well show up wearing a company logo golf shirt embroidered with these words: WE ARE ALL ABOUT OUR PRODUCTS! Hear me clearly: When you live by the product then you die by the product. Salespeople who lead with their offering are admitting that they bring zero value to the equation, and they're essentially telling customers to commoditize the purchase decision.

Salespeople Conducting Amateurish and Ineffective Sales Calls Are Dooming the Salesperson to Vendor or Product-Pitcher Status

Who's teaching salespeople how to plan and conduct sales calls? If what I'm seeing is any indication, nobody is. So much sales training today is focused on macro theories. Popular sales blogs and LinkedIn posts are filled with articles espousing the virtues of macro sales theories like social selling and insight selling. But there are few sales experts writing about how to better execute the day-to-day basics, the fundamentals. Talking about sales call structure may not be sexy, but it has never been more needed, especially as sales managers are spending less time in the field coaching people.

Here are some of the most common sales call sins:

► The salesperson doesn't establish herself as a professional or assert control by setting up the meeting, sharing her agenda, and getting buy-in from the customer.

► Sellers approach the sales call already in *presentation mode* and are too quick to jump to a demo or presentation.

► Salespeople talk way too much and listen way too little. It's very hard to come across as a professional problem solver when you don't *discover* the customer's real issues. As I'm fond of repeating: Discovery precedes presentation—always!

► Salespeople give off the vibe that they are there to "pitch at" the prospect, which creates an awkward, adversarial dynamic and often provokes a guarded, even cynical, posture from the customer.

Take some time now to replay in your mind the last dozen or so of your people's sales calls that you observed. Were the salespeople coming across as consultative professionals or product pushers? Did they do more talking or listening? Was their objective to learn as much as possible as to improve the customer's condition, or to launch into presentation mode as quickly as possible? And, most important, if you were the customer, how would you view the salesperson—simply as a self-interested vendor or as a true value creator, advisor, and trustworthy business partner?

Amateurish approaches doom the salesperson to vendor and product-pitcher status. You don't earn a seat as the expert or consultant at the customer's table when you're viewed as a pitchman better suited to doing infomercials than to helping your customer address business challenges.

Salespeople Doing Whatever the Customer Requests Come Across as Order Takers

When the customer or prospect tells a salesperson to jump, a majority respond with the traditional "How high?" and typically do so with great excitement. They think, what could be better? The customer wants me to do something and I will show him that I'm the best, I'm the fastest, I'm the most compliant, I have the best attitude, I follow instructions better than anyone, I'm likable, I present better than anyone, and I'll provide the most creative and in-depth proposal.

The super-responsive or highly relational salesperson is probably incredulous reading this, shaking his head in disbelief that I'd actually *go there*. Well, based on what I am seeing across a very wide variety of sales roles and industries, I have no choice but to *go there*. The harsh reality is that when the seller does whatever the customer asks and is more concerned with being liked than respected, it often lowers instead of raises the perception of the salesperson in the buyer's eyes. Sure, that sounds counterintuitive, but it's true.

Please don't read more into this than I'm writing. In no way am I declaring that responsiveness is unimportant. It's hugely important. And I'm not advocating that salespeople behave like obstinate unlikable jerks. Not at all. But I am strenuously making the case that in today's sales environment, where value is the yardstick by which all potential providers are measured, it is imperative that we think hard about how sellers are perceived by buyers. Too often, the very likable, highly relational, super-responsive, overly accommodating salesperson gets blown out of the water when going up against a true sales killer who owns his sales process and isn't afraid to push back against the buyer.

How do your people respond when a potential client they haven't been working summons them to come in for a *presentation* or *demo*, or announces that he's gathering his team together and wants their best dog and pony show? Do they get all lathered up, enthusiastically preparing for their big moment in the spotlight? Or do they raise one eyebrow, pause to think, and begin to wonder what prompted this prospect's request? Do they run headfirst and blind into this premature presentation, or do they assert control of the situation and begin an important dialogue with customer? Put bluntly, are they *yes men* (order takers) willing to do whatever a customer wants hoping to earn obedience points on the way to a sale? Or are they confident enough to push back on the request, professionally and respectfully informing the prospect that they'd loved to come in and present, but only at the right time, after having had the opportunity to meet various stakeholders, better understand what prompted the request, and learn more about the situation so they can then craft a relevant presentation?

Even more damaging and time consuming than premature presentations are premature proposals. How often is your sales team faced with the following scenario? A salesperson is on a first date with a prospect who appears to fall madly in love with your solution after only twenty minutes. The prospective client loudly exclaims how thrilled he is that your company pursued him, and he asks for a comprehensive proposal ASAP. Does your salesperson fall all over himself thanking the prospect for the opportunity and run back to the office to spend hours crafting the proposal? Or does he continue his probing in order to discover what's truly needed to write a good proposal and determine if this prospect is even qualified to buy from you?

How about this all-too-common situation: A sales team member receives a formal Request for Proposal (RFP) from a very large company that he has not been pursuing and where he has no relationships. Seems like we all face this quandary. Heck, even I do in my small consulting practice. A giant RFP for a massive sales training program shows up out of the blue from a company with which I have no relationship. It looks like my firm fits the requirements, and the thirty-page document should take about six hours to complete. Before I share how I respond, let me ask the real question: How often do you win those deals when your people simply comply and give the prospect what it requested? I can tell you how most of my clients answer that question in one word: Never! The same goes for me. In my entire twenty-five-year sales career I have never won a deal by responding to an RFP that I didn't know was coming. In fact, of the thousands of salespeople I've encountered, I have yet to meet a single one who has won a blind RFP that came in over the transom. Not one.

Let me close this chapter where we began. Ill-equipped salespeople are hurting sales and profit performance because they are consistently perceived by customers as nothing more than vendors. Contrary to what many weak salespeople believe, customers are not looking for subservient order takers; they are seeking help and value. And it's just about impossible to come across as a value creator when you're late to an opportunity, leading with product, pitching instead of probing, and presenting and proposing prematurely.

CHAPTER 16

Sales Leaders Chase Shiny New Toys Searching for the Magic Bullet

We're all suckers for the quick fix, and if those of us in sales leadership roles were truly honest, we'd have to admit that we might be the biggest suckers of all. Good sales leaders are all about return on effort and return on time. When we hear about a new methodology or tool promising more results with less effort, you better get out of our way, fast, because here we come in droves!

While sales leaders have likely always had this tendency, the danger (and resulting chaos) today is that new technology has enabled lighting-fast development, promotion, and proliferation of new tools and toys. The perpetual barrage of new sales ideas, theories, processes, and tools combined with the loud voices of the hucksters marketing them can overwhelm sales leaders. Many live in constant fear that they're going to miss out so they chase after shiny new toys hoping to find *the* magic bullet for all that ails in sales.

Don't Believe the Lie That Everything Has Changed

Over the past several years, we have heard a familiar refrain from those promoting the latest, greatest, hottest new thing in sales. The experts du jour are fond of telling everyone who will listen that *everything has changed*. Everything. *Nothing is the same*. Nothing.

What baffles me is how easily a darn large percentage of the sales population, including sales managers, is convinced that is true. Think about how ludicrous the assertion is. Everything has changed. Nothing that used to work in sales works anymore? Give me a break.

A few years back, when I was writing my first book, inbound marketing was all the rage. Many prominent voices in what was dubbed the Sales 2.0 movement boldly proclaimed the death of prospecting. These new sales "experts" cautioned us not to waste effort pursuing potential clients that had not given us permission to do so. They brashly predicted the end of sales as we knew it. According to the inbound marketing crowd, from that point forward in history, salespeople would become wildly successful responding to highly engaged and interested inbound leads who had been gobbling up content put out by their companies. If sellers perfectly followed these experts' prescriptions for content development and distribution and, of course, used their systems to track and respond to leads, there would be more opportunities to work than a sales team could handle. Ha!

More recently, social selling has dominated the headlines, sales blogosphere, and LinkedIn discussions. I've never witnessed a buzzword take an entire profession hostage like social selling has. Just do a Twitter search on #socialselling to get a feel for the incredible volume of tweets and nonsense being spewed on the subject.

A new set of "experts" has emerged, and because they are, well, social media experts, they've made an incredible amount of noise using various social platforms (Twitter, LinkedIn, Google+, and others) to build strong brands and large followings. Unlike inbound marketing, which was promoted by firms with offerings in the space, the banner for social selling is carried predominantly by individuals promoting their own names, content, and consulting. Social selling has become a cottage industry all its own.

Here's where it gets weird for me. In and of itself, social selling is a good thing. Using every available method to learn more about a prospect makes great sense. If there's an opportunity to connect on a social network, to be hanging out electronically where the prospects are, to plant a seed, to start a relationship, then by all means do it! Who wouldn't want to supplement their traditional selling efforts with new, fresh approaches? Every opportunity I get, I write or say that social selling (or inbound marketing or whatever the next shiny new sales toy ends up being) is a wonderful supplement to, but not a replacement for, traditional prospecting and new business development efforts.

I must have said enough positive things about the value of social media, or used it effectively enough in my own business, because in 2014 *Forbes* (in a study sponsored by KiteDesk) named me a Top 30 Social Sales Influencer and called me "one of the top 30 social salespeople in the world." What's ironic and somewhat amusing is that, since bestowed the honor of being named to that list, I've become a frequent outspoken critic of the one-trick-pony social selling pushers whose names also appear on the *Forbes* list.

Why do I rail so confidently against these "experts" as if I'm looking for a fight? Because I'm angry that these charlatans with their misleading hyperbole are hurting, instead of helping, people in sales. In the real world, in 100 percent of the companies I'm involved with on a daily basis, everything has not changed. In fact, just about *every* top-producing salesperson in *every* industry and *every* company is a master at the traditional aspects of selling that have *always* been critical for success. To drive home this point further, I'd love for these social sales "experts" to explain what struggling salespeople are supposed to do when inbound marketing and social selling don't provide a sufficient volume of leads to fill their pipeline. Since they are so quick to tell us that traditional prospecting is dead, what then should these desperate sellers do when the proposed magic bullet turns out not to be so magical after all?

Sales leaders, be wary of your tendency to chase after the next shiny new sales toy promising to alter the course of history. Believe me, I know it's hard to resist constant promotion—the banner ads, the email campaigns, the trade show sponsors, the webinar invitations. Almost every day I receive an email from a company with some new sales gimmick, gadget, or plug-in that promises to have the answer for what every one of my clients needs. I recently read a handful of articles packed with statistics on the proliferation of startups in the sales technology space. Thousands—that's right, not hundreds but thousands—of new companies are looking to sell us everything from sales force automation, sales enablement, and email tracking to browser plug-ins, CRM bolt-ons, and social selling integration. Each and every one of them promising a quick fix for your sales team. It's enough to make you scream. Or cry. Or, in my case, to see enough damage done to sales teams to be compelled to write this book.

Ignore the Fundamentals of Sales Management at Your Own Risk

As I wrap up the straight truth about why sales teams underperform in Part One and prepare to dive into the practical help offered in Part Two, let me share a profound realization that did not hit me until sitting down to write this chapter. Having worked with approximately 150 different sales organizations, I have yet to encounter a sales team that failed to deliver what was expected of them because they were missing some newfangled sales tool or process. Sales leaders and sales teams are not falling short of their revenue goals because they're being outsold by others deploying the latest and greatest toys and techniques. Quite to the contrary, sales teams underperform because sales leaders ignore or botch the very fundamentals of sales management.

Before forging ahead, let me ask you to consider spending time reflecting on the common causes of sales team underperformance outlined in these first sixteen chapters and assess which are potentially hindering your team's results:

- ► Lack of focus on goals and results

- ► Not publishing sales reports; sales managers not regularly reviewing results with individual members of the sales team

- ► Burying the sales manager with non-sales responsibilities

- ► Sales managers playing desk jockey or CRM jockey

- ► Managing the team via email and CRM screens

- ► Prioritizing CRM task management above sales results

- ► Player-coach selling sales managers trying to juggle opposite worlds

- ► Sales managers competing with their own people

- ► Sales managers with a hero complex deflating salespeople

- ► Sales managers losing sight of their primary job and replacing the battle helmet with a firefighter helmet, trying to personally tackle every problem

- ► Having the same person head up sales and operations and default to addressing urgent operational issues instead of pushing hard for sales growth

- ► A one-size-fits-all approach to talent management; poor role definition

- ► Asking farmers and engineers to pick up a weapon and become sales hunters

- ► Leadership turning a blind eye to perennial underperformers

- ► Silly, counterproductive compensation plans

► An anti-sales culture—arbitrary commission deductions, lack of appreciation, and constant complaining about salespeople

► High-ego senior executives who deflate the sales team by pontificating, micromanaging, and behaving inappropriately in front of customers

► Entrepreneurial, charismatic leaders who don't realize that their teams require more direction, clarity, and support to sell than they do

► Sales managers not mentoring and coaching on selling skills, or working in the field with salespeople

► Salespeople being perceived as nothing more than vendors or commodity sellers because they:

- Live in reactive mode and are not proactively pursuing prospective customers, and therefore arriving late to opportunities

- Lead with their product instead of the customer's issues

- Conduct amateurish and ineffective sales calls

- Do whatever customers request, including delivering premature presentations and proposals

► Sales leaders ignoring fundaments while perpetually chasing shiny new toys in search of the magic sales bullet

Note: The above list covers leadership reasons sales teams underperform. For reasons why individual salespeople fail to develop new business, please see Chapter 2 of *New Sales. Simplified.* There is a free download available at www.newsalescoach.com.

PART TWO

Practical Help and a Simple Framework to Get Exceptional Results from Your Sales Team

CHAPTER 17

A Simple Framework Provides Clarity to the Sales Manager

Thank you for plowing through my blunt observations in Part One on why so many sales teams struggle to deliver the desired results. Some of you may have already begun addressing topics and making changes based on what you've read so far, but I am acutely aware of your potential discomfort at having a mirror up held up so closely and being challenged by perspectives and opinions that are not very popular today. Believe me, I also realize the risks that can result from pointing the finger back at the very people who hire me. But these perspectives need to be shared.

If you're a senior executive or sales manager and were offended by what you've read, I apologize to you—kinda, sorta. The goal was not to offend or to put you in a defensive posture. My intention was to deliver a wake-up call. The motivation in offering so many blatant examples of sales mismanagement (or lack of management) was simple and pure: to help you identify the areas in your own sales organization that may be getting in the way of its success.

To kick off the second half of the book, let's break down sales management into its essential components and look at a very simple framework that has helped many companies get exceptional results from their sales teams.

Sales Management Is Not One Big Broad Issue

In many companies, "Sales" is looked at as one big issue. When things are not going well, people make blanket statements like "Sales is broken." Often, when I'm brought into a company whose sales team is underachieving, senior executives and sales leaders will express their frustration at being truly overwhelmed by the enormity of fixing "Sales." It's as if they want to attack the whole thing as one giant problem they're hoping to solve.

Reflecting back on my first experience as a sales manager, which I related in Chapter 1, I empathize with how these executives feel. I was overwhelmed to the point of exasperation. In many ways, the world seemed to be moving too fast and it seemed like I was under attack. All the individual issues I was fighting morphed into one massive challenge that felt like an enemy too big and too complex to conquer.

However, the reality, and the good news, is that "Sales" is not one thing. It's many disparate things all under one large umbrella. Here's just a partial list:

Culture. Energy. Accountability. Passion. Goals. Results. Leadership. Team dynamics. Team meetings. The manager-salesperson relationship. Focus. Competition. Role definition. Recruiting. Coaching. Skills development. Retaining top producers. Remediating or replacing underachievers. Field work. Compensation. The salesperson-customer relationship. Sales process. Strategic targeting. Prioritization. Prospecting. Probing. Presenting. Proposing. Pipeline management. Value creation. Negotiating. Business planning. Follow-up. Resilience. Perseverance. Emotional Quotient. Compensation. Culture.

As you read that list, you were likely thinking two things: First, that is one long list! And second, the list begins and ends with culture. Correct on both fronts.

Break Down Sales Management into These Three Clear Categories

When I set out to improve the health and effectiveness of a sales team, and ultimately increase sales, I deploy a very simple grid, a filter if you will, that helps sort the myriad of potential sales issues into three main buckets.

1. Sales Leadership and Culture

2. Talent Management

3. Sales Process

I view each of these buckets as essential pieces of the sales management framework. Beyond using this grid as a *lens* to guide my coaching and consulting, I also work hard to help clients adopt it as their own sales management framework. In other words, I go beyond simply using it myself to improve a sales organization. My bigger objective is for sales leaders to own this framework and to know with 100 percent certainty that if they focus on these three essential sales management categories, they'll see a marked improvement in their sales team and results.

Sales Leadership and Culture is where we start the *Sales Management. Simplified.* journey. The first dozen or so years of my sales career, I worked only in pro-sales environments. Unhealthy, unhelpful, and unproductive sales team cultures were a foreign concept to me. It wasn't until I took a job at a company with goofy sales leadership and a bizarre culture that I began to even ponder the effect of culture on sales performance. This was a necessary awakening, because I discovered over the past dozen years that those healthy cultures I benefited from early in my career were the exception, not the norm. In fact, it is so uncommon to stumble upon an extremely healthy sales culture that it is almost shocking when I do find one. Two years ago, I did a project for a firm outside Philadelphia that had the single healthiest culture I've encountered. It was so wonderful and so rare that I've been talking about it ever since. You'll read more about that company and its approach to sales leadership in Chapter 18.

I was also a bit slow on the uptake regarding the importance of leadership and culture in sales performance because I came into consulting as an expert sales technician mistakenly believing that if I coached the heck out of every individual salesperson and sales team, I could transform performance. Confident in my content and ability to persuade and coach, I naively ignored how the sales organization's leader and culture factored into the performance equation. Today, I laugh looking back at my youthful ignorance. I now believe that the team's leadership and culture are more critical to a business's sales success than are the skills of its producers.

"Leadership and Culture" may seem like a vague or general catchall phrase. Let me offer some questions to guide you down the path and to set the stage for upcoming chapters on this important first piece of the framework.

- ▶ What does it *feel* like to be part of your company's sales team?

- ▶ Is it a high-performance culture? Why do you feel that way?

- ▶ Are team members laser-focused on goals and results?

- ▶ What's the vibe in the sales department (whether it is local or based remotely)?

- ▶ What does *accountability* look like on this team?

- ▶ How often, how big, and how loud are victories celebrated?

- ▶ Is the manager leading the team or just reacting to circumstances?

➤ Are sales team meetings valuable? Do salespeople leave those meetings better equipped, envisioned, and energized, or drained and discouraged?

➤ Do members of the sales team feel supported, valued, and appreciated?

➤ Does the existing compensation plan make sense and does it drive the desired behaviors and results?

➤ In what ways is the manager putting his or her fingerprints on the team?

➤ How much of the sales leader's time is devoted to non-sales activities and executive and administrative burdens?

➤ What's the level of intensity, passion, and heart-engagement of team members?

I don't believe that anyone would doubt that we can create significant *lift* in a sales organization by improving the answers to these questions.

Talent Management is the next piece of the sales management puzzle. Senior executives and sales managers agree that talent is a huge issue. No one contests that assertion. Yet, while executives give lip service to giving talent management its due, lip service is often all it is. Some leaders have trouble tackling "sales talent" because they feel overwhelmed by the enormity of the task. The situation is similar to how "Sales" feels too big to attack; sales leaders tell me they're not sure where to even begin addressing talent management.

While working with a senior executive a few years ago, I created a mini-framework to help us better segment, strategize, and address the various talent deficiencies in her sales organization. Breaking talent management into the following four sub-categories was so beneficial on this project that I began using this process as my go-to model for all things sales talent. I call it the Four Rs of Sales Talent Management:

1. Right People in the Right Roles

2. Retain Top Producers

3. Remediate or Replace Underperformers (coach up or coach out)

4. Recruit

Sure, *remediate* isn't really the ideal word there, but I was looking for something easy to remember that kept with the alliteration. Each of the Rs is a major topic addressed in Chapter 23. But before we dive deeper to explore each element, my hope is that just seeing those four categories serves as a catalyst for you to begin gaining clarity on your sales talent issues and opportunities.

Sales Process, particularly new business development sales process, is my favorite piece of the sales management puzzle.

The truth is that I love sales. I bleed sales. For all the time I've now spent as an executive, as a consultant, and as a speaker, deep down I'm still a sales guy. I love the chase and the art of selling. Even when I'm drowning in work, I'll pursue a lead or referral because the competitor in me wants to win, and because I strongly believe that I'm the best solution for the prospective client. You see, I take my own medicine prescribed back in Chapter 7. Since I'm the guy who heads up both sales and operations for my firm, I am conscious not to take my foot off the gas and let the ops guy win—even when it appears that there is far more work than we need or want! I am unashamedly proud to be called a salesperson, and I love nothing more than helping other salespeople become more proficient sales hunters.

There are certain key sales management responsibilities when it comes to sales process. Managers must help point team members in the right direction to strategically target appropriate customers and prospects. After pointing the team, the manager ensures that the salespeople are armed with the necessary sales weapons and that they become proficient at using them. And because victory is dependent on successful execution at the point of attack, the manager must monitor the sales battle, checking that the troops are executing their plans and staying on course.

While sales process may be my favorite piece of the sales leadership framework, and the one that comes most naturally for me, it is also intentionally third in the order—squarely behind leadership and culture and talent management. Reiterating the perspective shared back in Chapter 1, during my first stint in consulting I learned from experience that you can't transform sales organizations by coaching everyone into better salespeople. To create meaningful, lasting sales performance improvement, it is critical to get sales leadership and culture and talent management right first.

CHAPTER 18

A Healthy Sales Culture
Changes Everything

Culture is not some soft, ethereal concept. Organizational culture is a big deal. It's such a big deal that famed author, speaker, and leadership guru Patrick Lencioni dedicated his latest book, *The Advantage* (San Francisco: Jossey-Bass, 2012), to it. Lencioni's blockbuster makes the case that what separates super-successful companies from mediocre ones is the health of the organization, not the brains. He asserts that healthy organizations outperform because they boast great clarity and sense of purpose, which creates an environment in which top performers not only thrive but never want to leave. Isn't that every executive's fantasy description for their sales team culture? It sure is mine.

Merriam-Webster defines culture as *"the set of shared attitudes, values, goals, and practices that characterizes an institution or organization."* Its less-formal definition describes culture as *"a way of thinking, behaving, or working that exists in a place or organization."* I find these definitions very helpful as I launch into defining a healthy sales culture. But first, I'd like to ask you to consider the following questions concerning your current sales team culture:

- What are the predominant *shared attitudes* across the sales organization, including the sales manager?

- Could your team members articulate agreed-upon *shared values?* If so, what are they?

- Which *shared practices* are hallmarks of your sales team?

- Is there is an accepted, understood, and enforced *way of thinking and behaving* that characterizes your salespeople?

Culture Matters

At the company where I first took a sales position (the large consumer products company where I worked for the indefatigable Bob Smith), the founder and CEO was really the chief salesperson. He understood sales and was pro-sales. His focus was top-line growth, and grow we did; sales took off like a rocket. It was a hoot to sell for this fast-moving company, and everyone in sales enjoyed the spoils of victory.

My second sales job was in a tiny family-held business. I went to work for a dear friend and fraternity brother. He headed up operations and the "back of the house" and entrusted me to run the front side of the business as head of sales. My friend had great instincts when it came to setting the tone and culture of our little sales organization. He was very clear on what he expected from me, as I was with him in terms of what support was necessary to grow the business. Every time I hit the road, I knew he had my back. And when I'd come up with a harebrained idea, instead of pooh-poohing it, he'd actually listen and try to help get me what was needed to win a deal or fill a vacuum in the marketplace. I *felt* totally supported in my sales role. I was appreciated, valued, and respected. But, don't for a second read more into that than I'm writing here. It wasn't easy, and he wasn't easy on me! Quite the opposite. My boss/friend was no pushover. In fact, he was constantly pushing for more: more appointments, more new markets, more new customers, more margin, more ideas—more everything. It was awesome. He perfectly balanced encouraging my heart and kicking my ass.

The disappointment from leaving my friend's business was short lived because it was at my next company where I discovered sales heaven and my career really took off. This company got just about every aspect of sales culture right. It had a powerful, pro-sales CEO, the most pro-sales CFO I've encountered, and a world-class sales manager (the aforementioned Donnie Williams, who later became my consulting partner). Donnie understood better than anyone how to balance making it fun while ramping up accountability. We had fun, energizing, and helpful sales team meetings. Salespeople wrote and presented annual business plans that became living documents. Sales reports were published and public. Everyone kept score and competed with each other to see who came out on top each month. Donnie regularly met one-on-one with each salesperson to review results and opportunities that were in the hopper. The compensation plan was smart and leveraged. Top producers made top dollar, and those who struggled felt the pain when commission checks were distributed. Even better, commission was based on gross margin, not revenue. So when a salesperson won big, it was because the company was also winning big. Commission and bonuses were delivered with smiles not resentment. Sales was king at this company; everyone knew it and everyone benefited from it.

It took fifteen years, four employers, and almost 150 consulting engagements until I found a company with a stronger sales culture. That's how amazing that company was, and what a treat it was to work there. Little did I know how spoiled I was or how unique that environment.

During those fifteen years I (un)fortunately had the opportunity to work for, observe, and consult for a wide variety of organizations with less-than-ideal sales cultures. A good number of those observations made their way into Part One of this book.

Pain can be a very good teacher. The first authentic anti-sales culture I encountered was at a software company with an enterprise learning management system that I joined just as the Internet bubble was bursting in 2000. It was my first real exposure to an executive team who truly didn't understand sales. This small company was run by entrepreneurial software guys, and the cubicles were filled with, you guessed it, software developers. It was so quiet in the office that the most audible sounds were mouse clicks and the crack and gas hissing from opening a soda can. Free soda and the monthly run to Sam's Club in the CEO's truck to replenish the soda fridge were probably the best parts of working there. Come to think of it, that says a lot, doesn't it?

One day my wife popped into the office to visit. Freaked out by the silence, she leaned over my desk and said in a hush, "What's wrong? Why is everyone so quiet? Did something bad happen?" I whispered back to her, "What's wrong is that I work for this company." And then I intentionally raised my voice loud enough to make a scene, "Nothing is wrong, hon. It's always this quiet in here!"

The silent office was the least of this company's sales culture issues. The executive team's fuzzy strategy, unclear direction, and dictated "demo-first-ask-questions-later" sales process were certainly bigger challenges. That combined with frenzied sales leaders who ran around with their hair on fire and wouldn't or couldn't offer clarity about which specific target markets the sales team should attack. Every day was painful. Every. Single. Day. Until I was fired. That was a great day that helped to propel me into the sales improvement business. More gory details about the abject sales failure of this company and how that experience set me up for success as a sales coach and consultant can be found in Chapter 4 of *New Sales. Simplified.*

As a consultant, I've been in company after company with less-than-ideal sales cultures. The reasons vary greatly. In one organization it's the heavy-handed CFO who doesn't even pretend to hide his jealousy of the sales team's compensation or his general animosity toward all things and all people sales related. In another it's the control freak president who will not allow the salespeople to make even the smallest decisions in their territories, insisting on approving every little promotional expense. In other organizations it's the project managers who specialize in accusing salespeople of "selling and dumping," and taking potshots at top producers for setting client expectations unreasonably high. There's the all-too-common blaming the sales team for poor results but deflecting the credit to any number of factors (the economy, the product, weak competition, luck, etc.) when they blow their numbers out of the water. And of course, there are the myriad of ways companies jerk around with sales compensation—territory changes, quota increases, commission deductions, and more.

In some organizations the unhealthy sales culture manifests itself in more subtle ways. In these cases, it's not a jealousy or dislike of sales, it's more a lack of appreciation for what the sales team is supposed to be doing to drive revenue. I see companies that regularly take advantage of what they perceive as a salesperson's "free time." Salespeople are often used as "free labor" to participate on projects, to assist those managing programs, to essentially help out customer service, operations, and other areas. The shame is that it's typically the weaker salespeople who best accommodate these requests. They're not bold, strong, confident, or outspoken enough to resist. The result? The salespeople who can least afford to sacrifice their "selling time" end up doing so the most, which, naturally, translates into even lower sales production. And then when the quarter ends, the same management assigning salespeople non-sales work turns back around to blame the salesperson for not hitting sales goals. That maddening scenario is more common than you might think, and beyond anything else, it is a culture issue. When the sales function is not respected bad things happen to sales results.

And, of course, there are the prominent unhelpful attitudes and behaviors of sales leaders and senior executives presented in Part One. I would ask you to scan the titles of Chapters 2 through 16 to refresh your memory of the various ways key leaders contribute to an unhealthy sales culture.

Everything Flows from Culture!

After all my whining about bad sales cultures and the people who create them, I imagine you're more than ready to see a list of characteristics of an ideal sales culture. So am I. But instead of just dropping an academic bulleted list on you here, it will be more powerful and beneficial to describe the absolute best sales culture I've ever seen.

As mentioned earlier, it took fifteen years and exposure to almost 150 organizations from the time I left the "sales heaven" company until I found another with a better, stronger, healthier sales culture. A couple of summers ago I received a call from a CEO named Robert. I liked Robert immediately. He was articulate, passionate, powerful, direct, and funny. Robert was quick to tell me that his company was killing it. It was hitting on all cylinders and experiencing significant revenue growth. Just that week, management took the entire sales team (of more than twenty people) to dinner and the Rolling Stones concert to celebrate their success. After hearing Robert speak even for just a few minutes, I immediately wanted to work with his company. I knew I could learn a ton from him and his company. However, I had one big question.

I told Robert that it was a treat to get a call from a company that was doing so well because 95 percent of the inbound inquiries I receive are from companies and sales leaders who *need* help. With a smile and inquisitive tone, I asked, "Robert, what prompted this call? It sounds more like I could use your help with some of my hardheaded CEO clients than you could use mine." He thanked me for the compliment and then blew me away with what came next. "Yes, we are doing exceptionally well. But we are always striving to improve. We've been reading your book as a sales team. Every week we review a chapter in our sales team meeting. It's been fantastic and stirred up all kinds of conversations and ideas. When we got to the chapter on sharpening our sales story, it seemed like it might be valuable to have you come in to personally help us."

Before I go any further recapping this story, my hope is that you are already getting a sense for the "leadership and culture" at Robert's company. I haven't even begun to share what it felt like when I walked through the company's front door, yet you already have a flavor of how strong the sales culture is from this one brief phone call: He leads. He pushes. They are serious about results and play to win. They celebrate. They have productive team meetings. They are hungry to improve. And, clearly they have great taste in books and consultants ☺.

We put together a small engagement that revolved mostly around improving the team's messaging as they pursued bigger prospects and higher-level contacts, and also some coaching on best practices for prospecting and presenting.

The first thirty minutes at this company's office was like going to sales fantasy camp. It was the equivalent of how I'd expect to feel visiting Porsche's factory in Stuttgart or possibly hanging out with Peyton Manning as he prepared for a big game. It was *that good* and that exciting. I visit a lot of companies and am pretty quick to get a feel for the emotional dynamics at play. The sales culture at this place was palpable. The energy was electric. The engaged faces and intense voices were refreshing. Everywhere I turned there were whiteboards charting some sales statistic, goal, or result. Did I mention that it was loud? That people were laughing? That I felt like I was visiting the winning locker room of a championship team? As a sales consultant, it was as if I was on holy ground. After just thirty minutes onsite, I knew I was experiencing something very special, something I hadn't seen for fifteen years.

I sat down in Robert's office and could tell he was aware of the impression his company was making on me. He told me a bit about his past and the backstory for launching the business. I noticed his shelves were filled with leadership and sports books about iconic coaches and lots of memorabilia. Robert described the annual goal-setting process he personally went through with each member of the sales team. He talked about the importance of knowing what makes each person tick and how his management team makes it a point to manage every person as an individual. He bragged about the extreme level of success a few of his producers were having and then circled back to fill in details of the intense coaching and mentoring required to help these individuals to raise their games. Again without prompting, he extolled the value of the regular manager to salesperson one-on-one meeting, where he saw it as the manager's job to better understand the salesperson, to review goals and results, to help remove obstacles, and to stretch the salesperson. He grabbed a rubber band off his desk and began to stretch it. He said that his job was to find out how far he could push each person, for his or her own good, without causing the person to break.

I'll admit it. I may have been drooling on myself just listening to Robert. I wish these types of conversations with owners, senior executives, and sales managers were more common. I really do. But they are not. It was a rare treat to be sitting with a "leadership and culture" expert who happened to be leading a sales team that was two to three times more productive per person than what is typical in his industry.

I knew that one day I'd be writing a sales management book with a chapter dedicated to the importance of a healthy sales culture. What I didn't expect was that I would get to observe all of the characteristics of an ideal culture in one client! This chapter was writing itself two years before I was ready to write the book!

I asked Robert to expand further about the power of his sales culture and shared my observations from the half-hour wandering around his office. Then I asked, "What is with the culture here? You can feel it."

Robert leaned forward and whispered, "Michael, everything flows from culture. Culture is everything." At that moment, I was ready to give back my fee because I would've done this engagement for free.

Robert spent another hour sharing his perspective and spoke of how he jealously guarded the culture at his company. He referred to the culture as the company's "secret sauce." He went on to explain the brutal interviewing and onboarding process for new hires. The management at his company was more concerned with repelling the wrong people (who wouldn't fit) than with hiring the very best talent available. In fact, much of the lengthy interview process was designed to scare away candidates. I can't tell you how different that approach is from what I see in so many companies with lame cultures.

I just recently sat in on a group interview for another client. Key executives and I were meeting with a candidate for whom we had mixed feelings. But fifteen minutes into the two-hour interview, the CEO interrupted our questions and started selling the candidate on joining his wonderful company. I mention that here only because the contrast is so striking between the one company with a phenomenal high-performance sales culture that strenuously screened every hire and this other company with an unhealthy sales culture whose leader chose to fill an empty chair with the warm body in front of him.

I spent the balance of that first day at Robert's company meeting individually with key producers and then had dinner with their very engaged management team. It was a blast, but the experience of day one paled in comparison to day two. The following day I spent about six hours facilitating a sales team meeting that only confirmed my initial thoughts about the firm's powerful culture. Sure, as planned, we sharpened the sales story and worked through how to incorporate elements of this improved messaging into the team's various prospecting and sales weapons. But what I'll never forget was the opportunity to watch the culture in action throughout the course of this meeting.

The communication in that meeting room was the most direct, transparent, blunt, confrontational, helpful, hysterically funny, loving, and healthy I've ever seen in any company for any type of meeting. This company used role play in ways I never thought possible. Sales team members were constantly needling each other, and management provided brutally honest feedback to salespeople throughout the day. At first, I was taken aback, even uncomfortable with the very direct communication style. But as the day wore on, I understood the fundamental reasons why such strong critiques and tough words were taken in stride, and I gained even more clarity about why this team was so outrageously successful. The good-natured teasing and brutal feedback was so well received because it was never personal; it was business, and on top of that, there was love and trust in the room. These very well compensated top-producing salespeople knew that management had their best interests at heart. After all, these were the same leaders who were meeting with them one-on-one, helping them to plan, to overcome obstacles, and to stretch themselves to production and income levels unheard of in their space. There was no doubt in that room that everyone was on the same team—from Robert to the management team to every producer. There were no hidden agendas or ulterior motives. Everyone knew that management was *for* the sales team, not against it. Sadly, that is rarer than you'd think.

The culture at this company truly was its key differentiator and competitive advantage. It also clearly dictated the *shared attitudes, values, goals, and practices* of the sales organization: We are elite. We strive to dominate the competition. We keep score and constantly look at and talk about the scoreboard—in the hallways, in our team meetings, and when we meet 1:1. We are loud and proud. We have each others' backs. We have fun. We are careful about who we add to this team because we have something very special and we guard it protectively. We come to team meetings with great attitudes, expecting to participate. We check our egos and pride at the door. We tease each other in a good-natured way because we're like family; we have very high standards and, most important, we want everyone to win. In fact, we expect to win. When we flop in practice we get called out because it is not acceptable to flop in the real game. We believe in pushing each other hard and telling each other the truth. And when we win big, we celebrate big.

No, "culture" is not a soft topic. As Robert so eloquently stated, everything flows from culture, and as you've read, the sales culture he's built is anything but soft.

Before moving on to look at how sales leaders must reallocate their time to more effectively lead their teams and to create the type of culture I'm advocating, take a few minutes to reflect on these important questions:

- How much more fun would it be—and how much faster could you create and maintain sales momentum—if your culture was like the wind at your back helping to drive sales growth instead of working against it?

- How much easier would it be to attract and retain top talent with a pro-sales culture?

- If I confidentially polled your salespeople, would the majority state that the leadership of your company is "for" the salespeople or against them?

- Is your current sales culture anything like what I described in my "sales heaven" job and at Robert's company, or are you light-years from that type of environment?

- How radical a shift in priorities and time allocation would it take to begin moving the sales culture needle in your organization?

CHAPTER 19

Sales Managers Must Radically Reallocate Their Time to Create a Winning Sales Culture

It's one thing to say you want a healthy, high-performance sales culture, but it's another thing altogether to do something about it. Fantasizing about how awesome it would be to have Robert's sales culture at your company won't make it happen. Frankly, I'll go as far as saying that unless you are willing to radically rethink and restructure how you (or your sales leader) spends your time, sadly, you won't make it past the fantasy stage.

The Sales Manager's Biggest Time Drains Hold Them Back from Leading Their Teams and Creating a Healthy Culture

I have a friend who's become an expert on the attributes of successful leaders and why certain executives are so much more productive than others. We got into a deep conversation about time wasters and how much time senior-level people spend on low-value tasks. I told him about a senior executive client of mine who was spending hours coordinating the travel and logistics for an upcoming corporate meeting. That led us down a path, and before long he was grilling me about how sales managers "invest" (waste) most of their time. Starting with email, I began to list their biggest time wasters. My friend immediately cut me off and declared, "Time Draculas. Travel planning and endless email in-box management. They suck a leader's time like Dracula." What a great word picture, and how right he was.

The topic of how sales managers allocate time was already burdening me. I felt like managers were unconsciously wasting endless quantities of time on low-payoff tasks and meetings. Inspired by my friend, I spent a couple of months paying particular attention to how sales managers at my current clients were actually "spending" time. Key word: *actually*. There is much lip service given to planning calendars and supposed sales management priorities. Best intentions are one thing, but reality is often another. After I closely observed a handful of managers across varying industries and company sizes, my initial suspicions were confirmed. As a whole, this disparate group of leaders not only spent their time in scarily similar ways but, unfortunately, spent it mostly in what I would consider low-value ways.

These are the five biggest time suckers/sins that keep sales managers from effectively leading their teams and creating the type of healthy culture described in Chapter 18:

1. They are slaves to email, perpetually checking and replying while living in reactive mode.

2. They sit in on a ridiculous number of meetings and conference calls that often have little to do with driving revenue—death by meeting!

3. They get caught up playing either Assistant GM or Firefighter-in-Chief.

4. They are buried with administrative and non-sales crap, get

asked to create or plow throw an obscene number of reports, and live with their heads constantly buried in CRM screens.

5. They don't *own* their calendars, protect their priorities, or plan well.

My hope is that this list of management time sins deeply disturbs you. Honestly, it's not worth the space or your time to further unpack these items. They're self-explanatory; most were addressed in Part One, and you know exactly what I'm referring to and how guilty you (or your sales manager) are of committing these sins. I list them here to drive home one big point: When sales leaders, either by force or choice, spend most of their working hours in these areas, by default they are not leading their teams, not building a winning sales culture, and certainly not driving new revenue for the company.

Save your rebuttal; I'm not interested. Instead of offering your rationale for why you *have to* devote so much time to non–sales leadership, non–revenue producing activities, maybe you should ask if there's a causal relationship between where you invest your time and the sales culture and performance of your team. I would argue that there most certainly is.

Feel free to call me an idiot who doesn't "get it," or doesn't understand your business, or how much work needs to get done. Believe me, I've heard it all before. To borrow from the great Jack Nicholson as Col. Nathan Jessup on the witness stand in *A Few Good Men*, truthfully, I don't give a damn how much work you think needs to get done! You want the truth? Whether you're the senior executive or the sales manager or play both roles, hear me clearly as if I was shouting this while turning red with veins bulging from my neck: When you're blasted with over 200 emails per day; trapped in meetings that keep you from your primary job; constantly handed (or grabbing for) the fire hose to deal with crises; buried either writing, reading, or scrambling for reports; and have almost zero control of your calendar, you are not leading anyone anywhere. Furthermore, you have exactly the sales culture you deserve—the one you've created, whether by design or neglect.

Just as we have no trouble bluntly informing the struggling salesperson that it's not about how busy he is or how hard he's working but that he gets paid to increase sales, sales leaders must preach that message to themselves! Somehow, some way, too many organizations have completely lost sight of the sales leader's mission. There are only so many hours in a week, and when those hours are consumed by *work* that doesn't contribute to leading the team, driving revenue, or enhancing the sales culture, then it's really hard to see how that's the best use of a sales leader's time.

The Sales Manager's Highest-Value Activities Should Be Obvious (but Read This Section Just in Case)

I understand that the last section may have caused some sales managers to throw this book against the wall. I get it. Some are angry with me because they don't appreciate the blunt, accusatory, unapologetic manner in which I presented it, and others are probably deeply frustrated with what feels like an insurmountable situation at their company. I understand. My goal is not to cause you heartache; it's to help you. And I have good news: It doesn't have to be like this. There is no law against good sales management. You are free to change your approach, behavior, and, most important, how you choose to spend your time. I know you will have to swim against the current, and fight against tradition, against the existing culture, and maybe against truly clueless executives with bizarre views of the sales manager's job. But I promise you that it's worth the fight.

The battle begins by acknowledging that in order to create the healthy, winning sales culture you so badly want, you must commit to radically altering where you spend your time. In fact, I'd go as far as to say that the sales leadership and culture battle is begun *and* won when you successfully transition to spending the majority of your time in high-value, high-payoff sales leadership activities.

So, what are these mysterious sales leader highest-value activities? Let's start with these three favorites:

1. Conducting one-on-one meetings with individual salespeople

2. Leading sales team meetings

3. Working alongside (observing, coaching, helping) salespeople when they are with customers and prospects

Is this list patently obvious? Probably. But you'd never know it if you logged how most sales managers spend their time. Sure, they'd give lip service to the importance of these critical activities, but their calendars would tell a very different story.

Going back to my simple framework for sales lift, in order to create sustainable sales performance improvement, we must improve the company's sales culture and how the team is led, the way sales talent is managed, and the sales process. The best way to attack these essentials is to meet individually with members of the team, meet with the team as a whole, and invest time working alongside salespeople in front of real customers and prospects.

The next three chapters dive into each of these critical sales management activities.

CHAPTER 20

Regular 1:1 Results-Focused Meetings Between the Sales Manager and Each Salesperson Will Transform Your Sales Culture

I am fully aware that upon seeing this chapter's title, many of you will think, "Thank you, Captain Obvious." Before you dismiss this topic and move on, please believe me when I write that this stupidly simple, über powerful, sales management best practice has the potential to transform your culture.

In every coaching relationship, I intentionally ask the sales manager a very simple, yet slightly vague question: How often do you formally meet 1:1 with each of your people? Invariably, I get an assortment of responses, but they typically include some version of the manager proudly sharing that she's in regular contact with her people. She'll tell me she speaks or emails with just about everyone *all the time*. I'll respond by saying that it's great that she keeps up with the troops, and then narrow down my question: "Let me be a bit more specific. How often do you have a formal scheduled meeting (either by phone or face-to-face) with each salesperson specifically to review their results and their pipeline of future sales opportunities?" That response doesn't come quite as fast and usually involves a bit of stuttering combined with a lengthy circular answer.

The Monthly 1:1 Meeting Was Modeled for Me

Until a few years ago, I had no idea that sales managers were not having regular (monthly) 1:1 meetings with their salespeople. Because early in my career managers did this with me, I mistakenly assumed that *every* manager was laser-focused on goals and results, and made it a point to review numbers with the people on their teams. I was shocked and dismayed to discover that this type of meeting was more the exception than a widely adopted practice. Frankly, twelve years into consulting, I am still amazed at how few managers do this and the even fewer who do it well. Isn't creating a results-focused culture and holding people accountable to hit sales goals Job Number One for any sales manager?

There are two huge reasons I have such strong convictions about this issue. First, as the salesperson, I benefited tremendously from having to sit down with my manager each month to face the music. And, second, I've observed sales leaders dramatically shift the culture and performance of their teams by instituting this simple type of meeting I am about to describe.

No head of sales executed this monthly 1:1 meeting better than Donnie Williams. Back in what now seems like the stone ages of selling (the late 1990s), Donnie was the vice president of sales in that company I mentioned earlier with the "sales heaven" culture. The commercial Internet was in its infancy. The "cloud," as we know it today, was still science fiction. Act! and GoldMine were the predominant contact management/sales tracking tools and precursors to today's robust CRM platforms. Donnie was old school and no fan of fancy software. He could read a spreadsheet but wasn't about to build one in Excel. So, the four tools Donnie used best in his monthly 1:1s were a pen, a yellow legal pad, last month's sales report, and his cheaters (reading glasses).

Sometimes the 1:1 would take place in Donnie's office, but most months he'd come sauntering down to mine. With a big smile on his face, the notorious yellow pad in hand, and his reading glasses way down on the end of his nose, he'd sit across from my desk. Before getting any further into this story, it's important to note that I was the top-producing salesperson of fifteen at this company. I mention that not to brag, but to make the point about how seriously Donnie took these 1:1 meetings. If there was anyone on the sales team who didn't need to be reminded about results or have his pipeline examined with a microscope, it was me. Now I ask you to pay careful attention to the *very* intentional manner in which Donnie conducted this meeting.

Peering at me over the top of his reading glasses, he always started by asking, "Mike, how are you doing?" Before my lips could form one syllable, Donnie would extend his left hand with his index finger up, and shake his head to stop me from answering. He'd look down at the sales report and then launch. "Actually, *let me tell you* how you are doing. Last month you booked $620,000, but your goal for the month was $700,000. Decent month, but what happened? Just a few weeks ago you were dead confident you'd blow that $700K number away." He'd pause, engage me in a very brief exchange, and then continue. "Year-to-date, you're at $4.2 million against your goal of $3.7 million, and for the year, you're ranked first in total sales but only ranked third on the team in terms of percent of goal achieved at 113.5 percent."

Every single month this meeting began exactly the same way. The sales leader and the salesperson both knew that before anything else, we were going to look at last month and year-to-date results versus goal and relative ranking versus the rest of the sales team. If the previous month and year-to-date results were phenomenal, the meeting was essentially over. Donnie would pat you on the back, tell you to keep it up, and then encourage you to go buy that fancy new car you'd been eyeing. Meeting adjourned.

But the reality is that the meeting almost never ended after the results phase. In the example above, sure I was doing pretty darn well, but I had missed the month and was trailing two other salespeople who were beating their goal for the year by more than I was. Donnie wasn't going to let me off that easy. "Mike, you missed the mark last month and it cost you. You've fallen to third in the rankings. What are you going to do about it?" Out came the legal pad with his notes from last month's meeting. "Where are you on these deals that didn't close last month as projected? What else is hot? Tell me what materialized from your Memphis trip last week? Take me through your most significant opportunities; let's talk dates and likelihood of closing."

Sure, today we have slicker tools, we communicate much faster, and everyone is kept better abreast of the status of deals in the pipeline. But don't let that distract you from the bigger point here. When the results weren't what they should've been, Donnie dug into the pipeline. If he liked what he heard from me—in other words, if my pipeline was healthy and it appeared to have sufficient volume and movement of opportunities to exceed my goals in upcoming months— he was satisfied and the meeting would then be over.

However, if Donnie was not pleased with the condition of the pipeline, then it was time for the third and least pleasant phase of the 1:1 sales manager meeting with the salesperson. No one liked it when it got to that part of the meeting. "Mike, results aren't what we need them to be, and your pipeline is weak. We both know there are not enough good opportunities to produce the revenue you need over the next few months. You've left me no choice but to ask: What the heck have you been doing? Grab your calendar. What was your activity last month? How many meetings did you have? What does next week look like and the week after? Let's pull out your business plan. Are you hitting the levels of activity you committed to hit? Who are you targeting right now and what are you doing to fill your pipeline and get sales back on track? I'm here to help. Is something in your way?"

This Sales Accountability Progression Is Good Management, Not Micromanagement

I've experienced that 1:1 results-focused sales manager–salesperson interaction from three angles. First, I benefited from being a well-managed salesperson. Having to face my manager every month showed me what this meeting, when done well, could do for the salesperson. Later, as Donnie's consulting partner, I benefited by observing him coach our client sales leaders on the importance of regular 1:1s with every team member. Finally, over the past ten years I've witnessed the transformational power these regular, formal, scheduled, results-focused sales manager–salesperson meetings have had on my clients' sales cultures. These meetings have such an impact on culture and performance that often months after concluding an engagement, a sales leader will contact me to share how implementing this one simple practice significantly improved her effectiveness as a manager and the results-focus of her team.

What makes this simple twenty-minute meeting so effective? To answer that, let's go back and deconstruct the phases and progression of the meeting.

THE SALES MANAGEMENT ACCOUNTABILITY PROGRESSION

1. Results

2. Pipeline

3. Activity

It's not just that these are the right elements for a regular 1:1. There is some magic in the order. The progression matters—a lot. Why? Because nobody likes to be micromanaged, and it's not fun having your boss ask you about your activity. Sure, we all know that key activity metrics are important. As I've stated earlier, I'm a big proponent of a high-frequency sales attack. In my experience, it's typically the salesperson who turns over the most rocks who finds the most opportunities. But when it comes managing the salesperson, there are several good reasons activity is not the place we want to start.

Results is the first phase in the accountability progression because, well, sales is all about results. It's that simple. I have repeatedly referred to this as a "results-focused" 1:1 intentionally. As leaders, if we want to build and maintain a results-focused sales culture, then we had better be talking about results every opportunity we get. Frankly, our people should tire of hearing us talk about results.

Something else wonderful happens, too, when we lead with results. It stops all the nonsense and bullshit that salespeople love to throw out at managers attempting to hold them accountable. Not sure about you, but I lose my patience very quickly when underperforming sales reps create a verbal smokescreen hoping to confuse and baffle sales managers with *everything* they've got going. Salespeople not hitting quota tend to get really good at dazzling their manager by reciting *all* the opportunities they're working. These 1:1s I'm advocating are not deal strategy meetings. They're not catch-up sessions. Their main purpose is to review past results and ensure that the salesperson will have good future results. Period.

In my opinion, 1:1 is the best venue for accountability. Sure, we are still going to publish, post, and distribute sales reports. And we will look at these reports in sales team meetings. If those not making numbers and ranked toward the bottom of the report are uncomfortable with that, good; they should be. But I'm not a fan of shaming or embarrassing people by calling out their poor performance in front of others, or having those who are struggling explain their results publicly. That creates an awful, negative, and demoralizing environment. In-your-face results accountability best takes place in a private session. That's why it's unfortunate that so few managers conduct this type of 1:1 today. Hence, the lack of accountability for results we see in so many organizations.

Starting off these meetings by reviewing results provides other benefits as well. When done regularly and properly, these meetings need not be overly emotional. I work with some managers who tend to shy away from hard conversations and the potential conflict that may arise during an accountability meeting. What I love about this type of 1:1 meeting, and specifically about starting with results, is that these meetings shouldn't be emotional or dramatic at all. There is no need to raise voices, use profanity, flail our arms, or make bold threatening statements. Nope. No histrionics required. We simply pull out the sales report and review actual results. Results for the month (or whatever finite period makes sense for your business). Results year-to-date. Relative results and ranking compared to the salesperson's peers. Just the facts, ma'am, just the facts.

Once we've reviewed the salesperson's past results, it makes sense that the next phase of this meeting should look at future results. Obviously we can't change the past, but we certainly can affect the future. The second phase of this suggested accountability progression is to do a quick, joint review of the salesperson's pipeline. I use the word *pipeline* in a broad sense here. Pipeline, to me, means potential deals or sales opportunities that are currently in this salesperson's funnel. Again, I don't want this "results-focused" meeting devolving into a long deal strategy discussion or coaching session. That isn't my intention. The main goal in this phase of the progression is to get a handle on the general health of the salesperson's pipeline.

The big question I am looking to answer is whether this salesperson has enough going on—enough deals in the hopper—for her to hit her sales goals in upcoming months. So from a macro perspective, I'm looking at the number of opportunities, their stage in the sales cycle, the dollar volume, and the likelihood they'll close. I intentionally used the words *quick* and *joint* to describe this phase of the meeting. Again, we are not looking to do a deep dive into the status of every opportunity. We simply want to review the overall health of the individual pipeline *with* each salesperson. In just a minute, I'll offer you two of my favorite questions to pose when you're really looking to ramp up accountability and better judge a sales rep's effectiveness quickly.

If we like what we see and are pretty confident that this salesperson has a robust funnel filled with a sufficient number of opportunities, it's time to wrap up the meeting and offer a few closing comments.

However, if after having reviewed this salesperson's less-than-stellar results, and now having found her personal pipeline rather anemic, it is time to move on to phase three of the sales management accountability progression: activity. The reality is that there is nowhere else to go as the manager. The salesperson with poor results and a weak pipeline is forcing you to ask hard questions about her activity level and how she is spending her time.

Before jumping in further on sales activity, let me address something you may be thinking about. I recognize that there might be a talent fit question about this underperforming salesperson. And sometimes it's not a talent issue, but more of a skills deficiency that requires training or coaching. Those are real possibilities and topics that will be addressed in later chapters. Remember though, for now, we are still talking exclusively about sales leadership and culture. I am intentionally remaining focused on results and accountability, not looking to problem solve. Yes, causes for underperformance need to be explored, but I firmly believe that this formal 1:1 meeting works best when its sole purpose is forcing the manager and the salesperson to confront the salesperson's results, pipeline, and activity. Too often, when sales managers and salespeople get together, the meeting gets sidetracked with ancillary topics, philosophical sales conversation, and excuses. As managers, it's our job to prevent that from happening.

The typical salesperson, and the struggling one even more so, does not enjoy getting the third degree about sales activity. No one likes to have his or her work ethic questioned. It doesn't feel good to be asked how many calls you made, appointments you had, or where you spent your time. That is why it is absolutely imperative that we start the progression by reviewing results, and when results are not what they should be, then we move to the pipeline. When accountability progresses in that order, all but the selectively blind and deaf self-protective salespeople understand that managers have no choice but to ask about activity. It's logical. It's our job.

Still, some underperformers will make a stink when questioned about their calendars and activity. They get defensive. Some go on the attack. Others have a premade, rehearsed list of excuses ready to roll off their tongues. They are prepared to defend their lack of activity before we even start asking about it. That alone should tell us something, shouldn't it?

Underperformers are quick to tell us that they don't do well when they are micromanaged. In response, I have a message for you, the sales manager, and another message for the salesperson who chooses to play the micromanagement card: First, to the manager, let's be crystal clear. This is not micromanagement. When results are poor and the pipeline is weak, asking a salesperson about activity is simply good management, not micromanagement. Don't for a minute let a struggling, defensive salesperson manipulate you into believing otherwise. And to the salesperson attempting to tell us you don't perform well when being "micromanaged," I say this: It doesn't look like you were doing too well on your own before we stepped in attempting to help you. So if you don't want to have these deeper level accountability conversations, there are two options. You can improve results and the quality of your pipeline so we don't need to talk about activity. Or, alternatively, you can go work somewhere else where they're cool with you failing.

Asking Just Two Questions Will Help You Quickly Weigh a Salesperson's Effectiveness

A few years ago, I was helping a company attempting to turn its reactive regional territory managers into proactive, new business development–focused salespeople. It was not an easy engagement. The company had a long history of tolerating underperformance. The sales executive had a "niceness" issue. He was truly a sweet man—too sweet. The company had survived the horrific downturn of 2008 through 2010, but during that time it did away with whatever little accountability was in place for the sales team. Two years later, the economy had rebounded but sales leadership was still rather complacent when it came to holding team members accountable to deliver results.

The CEO was committed to changing the culture, raising the bar on what was expected of the sales team, and sending a clear message about accountability for results. I invested some time coaching various managers how to conduct the type of 1:1 described in this chapter with their local territory managers. After a couple of months, I realized it was not working. The members of this seasoned sales team were masters at finger pointing, appearing busy, and making excuses. They were also slippery and really good at taking control of these 1:1 meetings. The managers trying to hold the salespeople accountable were getting a load of crap thrown at them and were too inexperienced to respond effectively. I made the decision to jump into the fray and conduct these 1:1 meetings with every territory manager myself for two consecutive months. My hope was twofold. First, I'd prove to the sales team that it truly was a new day and that the CEO was dead serious about accountability. Second, by having sales managers sit in on these monthly accountability meetings with the salesperson and me (either on the phone or in the room), they would pick up some of my approach and the questions I asked to cut through the crap and get to the truth.

When playing surrogate sales manager, I don't have the time or patience to let salespeople go on and on blowing smoke during accountability meetings. They quickly learn my preferred pace and process for accountability. We spend about two minutes talking about the sales report and results before I jump into reviewing progress in their personal pipelines. I then review their pipeline in whatever format that company uses and ask a few key questions to ensure that I have a good feel for what business is coming down the pike. And then I ask these two critical questions to get a very fast snapshot of how effective this particular salesperson is:

1. Can you name for me the new opportunities that are in your pipeline today that were not here when we met last month? In other words, can you tell me what fresh opportunities you have identified or created in the past month?

2. Can you name for me the existing opportunities that you moved forward in the sales process since we reviewed your pipeline together last month?

These two questions not only send a very direct message to the person with whom you're meeting, but also prevent the salesperson from burying you with bullshit in hopes you won't notice how ineffective or unproductive the last month has been!

If you ask a particular salesperson these two questions three months in a row, you get a very good handle how (in)effective he is at both creating new opportunities and advancing existing sales opportunities. In the months I played surrogate sales manager for this client, we not only set a new standard for what accountability should look like, we were able to rapidly make talent decisions about members of the team who clearly were not getting it done. I'll offer tips for coaching up or coaching out underperformers in Chapter 23, but for now, it's fair to conclude that you can get a pretty good feel for someone on your team by getting clear answers to these two questions in consecutive months.

Play out this scenario with me. You commit to holding monthly 1:1 meetings using the suggested accountability progression with everyone on your team. You'll meet face-to-face with local people and by phone with those based in other cities. In month one, Johnny the underperformer is dazed and confused by your direct approach. After you paint the big picture for him, he comes around to see that you are not evil or out to get him. You're just trying to help him succeed by confronting him with his results, reviewing his pipeline, and letting him see his progress creating new opportunities and moving others forward.

In month two, Johnny comes to the 1:1 armed with a long list of all the things he's got going, though none meet your criteria yet for a *real opportunity*. He starts to babble and you stop him to ask your two power questions. He freezes and then admits he hasn't opened a new opportunity this month and he has only excuses for why other deals haven't progressed.

In month three, you sit down with Johnny. This is now the third consecutive month in which you start with results and he has missed his numbers. You move to the pipeline phase of the accountability progression and don't like what you see. So you ask Johnny the two questions. Yet again, he hasn't added a thing to his funnel and has barely moved one opportunity forward.

Now it's my turn to ask you a question: How many more months do you need to have this conversation with Johnny?

My hope is that you can see how this one über-simple sales management practice can help transform your culture. I have seen it happen time and time again, and that's why I have little tolerance for executives and managers who declare there are more important tasks than formally meeting 1:1 with every salesperson on a regular basis. I vehemently disagree; this may be the single most important task on your plate.

CHAPTER 21

Productive Sales Meetings Align, Equip, and Energize the Team

Sales team meetings are critical to building a winning culture. They foster competition, cast vision, share best practices, challenge the team, conduct training (sales or product), build relationships between team members, and allow salespeople to see that they are part of something bigger than just themselves and their own territory.

I have participated in or observed what seems like countless sales team meetings. Some are wonderful. Many made me squirm in discomfort. I've been part of a few I'd rather forget (see Chapter 12). Lately, I have also noticed a trend in several smaller and midsize companies. They have stopped holding sales meetings altogether. It sounds odd, doesn't it? No weekly meeting or conference call. No monthly meeting. No big annual meeting. Nada. Nothing.

Sure, sales meetings take work, energy, and time to plan. And some of these companies have intriguing reasons why they've gotten away from gathering their salespeople together. But if the sales leader's mission is to create and foster a healthy sales culture, or possibly even turn around a sales team's performance, then team meetings are an important component of making that happen.

There Are Simple Reasons Sales Meetings Miss the Mark

Sales managers should not dread leading regular team meetings, and salespeople should not see it as drudgery to attend. Far from it. Our goal should be that both managers and salespeople alike should look forward to sales meetings. Crazy thought, I know.

There are a host of simple reasons why sales meetings miss the mark. At some companies, the meetings have no stated purpose. People aren't even sure what the objectives are or why they are there in the first place. Honestly, who wants to attend a meeting with nebulous goals? No one, that's who. In other cases, there is zero respect for time. Salespeople wander in or join the call late. Worse, the manager shows up late claiming he was "tied up" with an important matter. Worse still is when meetings do not conclude at their scheduled end time. It's hard to respect the meeting or the manager when there is no respect shown toward the attendees.

In addition, salespeople can demean team meetings in not-so-subtle ways. Many come in with sour attitudes. Others are distracted. As it has become fashionable to say lately, they are present but they're not present. Their bodies are in the room or on the call, but their hearts and minds are not. They continue playing on their smartphones, checking email, updating social media, or "working" a customer issue.

There is also an interesting group dynamic that tends to occur when salespeople come together. Instead of using their outspoken personas for good, they turn these gatherings into bitch sessions. One person makes a complaint (often an excuse couched as a complaint), and others smell blood in the water. Before long, it becomes a feeding frenzy of negativity. I'm all for direct conversation and making needs known to management. But too often these bitch sessions are unproductive, get out of control, and are allowed to go on for way too long.

One of my biggest recent complaints about client sales team meetings is that they're not sales meetings. Oh, the sales team is meeting, but it sure sounds and feels more like a project status meeting, a delivery scheduling meeting, or an executive strategy meeting. Late last year, I was visiting several regional offices to assess sales management health for a large client. In office after office, I sat through painful "sales" meetings, many of which went for hours. The length of the meeting wasn't the biggest problem, however. It was that only about 20 percent of the time was devoted to sales! The entire sales team was forced to sit through conversations about inventory levels, service issues, and the status of custom projects. Friends, that is not a sales meeting; that's an operations meeting from which no salesperson is walking out with more energy than he or she walked in with.

While on the topic of a salesperson's energy, let me address something I've touched on in passing. Team meetings are not the appropriate venue to beat up individuals. My personal goal is for every salesperson to leave the team meeting better equipped and more energized to do their job. Save the hard conversations for the 1:1s we reviewed in the previous chapter. Is it acceptable to yell at the team or for the manager to express disappointment with results, attitudes, lack of professionalism, or other issues? By all means, yes it is. A team scolding is one thing, but calling out, berating, and embarrassing an individual is another.

The final reason for less-than-ideal sales meetings is that the sales manager carries too much of the burden. He does all the planning and prep work and then also plays host, facilitator, teacher, trainer, and motivator during the meeting. That's crazy. Nowhere is it written that the manager needs to carry that entire load by himself. Just as on a good sales call, where the salesperson is speaking only a third of the time, sales team meetings shouldn't be monologues conducted by the manager. He's the quarterback who calls the plays and *owns* the meeting, but that does not mean he should play lineman, receiver, running back, and water boy, too. He can and should distribute the prep work and content that will be presented at meetings.

Try This Menu of Potential Agenda Topics to Spice up Your Team Meeting

By far, the most common request I receive for help with sales meetings is with agenda topics. Sales managers are craving ideas to make their team meetings more meaningful. Here are some of my favorite agenda items:

> ► *Personal Updates.* Go around the horn asking each person to share for a minute or two what's going on in his or her personal life. It's a great opportunity to enhance relationships on the team and to build empathy. When people are transparent, we may discover important news in a team member's life that helps us better understand why the person is moody, grumpy, elated, distracted, etc. If someone's kid is really struggling or he's dealing with a terminally ill parent, wouldn't that be valuable to know? On the flip side, if the top producer announces that she's buying a summer home on the lake, wouldn't that serve as good motivation for the rookies on the team?

> ► *Review Sales Results and Highlight Outstanding Performance.* While I've made the case that we should scold individuals in private, we should definitely celebrate success in public! The sales meeting is a great place to distribute and review sales reports. Give the top producers their due. Highlight outstanding individual achievements or marked improvement. Be generous with praise.

> ► *Success Stories.* Ask a handful of salespeople to share the specifics about a recent sales victory. You can either ask the individuals to come to the meeting prepared, providing guidelines about what and how long you'd like them to present to the team, or you can spring the request right at the meeting. Just pick out a few salespeople and ask them to tell the story of

how they won a certain piece of business. Tell them it's permissible to brag about their sales heroics, and that the more specifics they can give, the more everyone else will benefit.

▶ *Product Training.* There's always room for improvement. Could your people use a refresher on something they've been selling for a while? Or are you launching a new product or service that requires the team to be trained?

▶ *Best Practice Sharing.* This is one of the very best ways to share the content load with your team. Rotate through various team members over the course of several meetings. Do you have someone who is a master at getting appointments by phone? A rep who is incredible at penetrating and cross-selling? Someone who shows up every day with a kick in her step and a smile on her face? Pick a team member to prepare a ten-minute segment to share his or her best practice at the meeting. Peers will get a ton of value from it and it's zero work for the manager!

▶ *Deal Strategy Brainstorming Session.* None of us is as smart as all of us. Do you want to put the power of your team to good use? Right in the meeting ask team members to bring up a sales situation in which they are stuck. Have a salesperson tell the story of how the opportunity ended up where it is, what he has done thus far, and why he thinks the deal is stuck. Then go around having other people ask tough questions to better diagnose the situation. Once the questions have all been asked, get everyone's best suggestions on how the salesperson with the stuck deal should proceed. I guarantee you the entire team benefits from this.

▶ *Executive or Other Department Guest Presentation.* Have an executive or key person from another department spend a half-hour at your sales meeting. A senior finance person could breakdown the P&L statement or share something interesting about banking relationships, or how taxes and regulations impact the business. Bring in an engineer or R&D person to tease the team with some exciting new solution being created.

► *Book or Blog Review.* Read a book together as a team. Discuss a chapter or two at each sales meeting. Assign a salesperson to lead the discussion each week so she comes prepared. If a book seems like too much to digest, send out a link to a sales blog post that you like and have the team come ready to discuss it. Even better, assign a different team member this task for every sales meeting so you don't have to.

► *Sales Skill Coaching/Training.* This can be done by the manager or you can bring in an outside expert, but it needs to happen occasionally. Way too much sales meeting time is wasted on non-sales topics and too little is spent sharpening the sales skills of the team. Carve out time to review the basics, like prospecting by phone, conducting effective sales calls, asking great probing questions, and delivering presentations.

► *Business Plan Presentations (or Reviews).* Individual business plans are powerful tools for the salesperson and a gift to the sales manager. Have salespeople prepare and present their annual individual business plan to the team. Or, if you've done that already, have them do a midyear review of how well their plan is working and how closely they've followed it. Much more on business plans to come in Chapter 26.

► *Brief, Controlled Bitch Session.* As ugly as an all-out bitch session might be, sometimes allowing team members to point out obstacles impeding their success can be very productive if done in a positive, controlled way. Every so often, allow for a brief "airing of grievances" (Frank Costanza's Festivus *Seinfeld* episode) where salespeople can vent about silly policies or point out areas where they feel unsupported or ill-equipped. Management can score major points by listening, and even

145

more points for successfully addressing an issue the team brings up and removing that obstacle.

► *Non-Sales-Related Inspiration.* Watch a powerful movie clip. Read an inspiring story about someone who beat cancer. Have team members bring in a picture of something that keeps them motivated. Bring a local war hero veteran in to tell his story.

► *Takeaways.* At the conclusion of the meeting, have people share their two big takeaways—one thing they learned or that they can incorporate immediately, and another that will require some time and work on their end to implement.

I hope this list will serve as a catalyst for those looking for a few fresh ideas. By no means is it intended to be exhaustive. There are many other productive topics that can be covered in team meetings. Earlier, I told the story of how one particular client extensively used role play as a development tool with phenomenal results. If the environment is conducive and the culture is "safe," role play can serve as a great way for salespeople to practice new techniques and increase their effectiveness when facing live prospects and customers.

Team Meetings Provide an Opportunity for the Sales Leader to Set the Tone

Your sales meeting may be your best opportunity as the leader to set the tone for your team. What you communicate has a huge impact on *your* sales culture. Your physical appearance, voice inflection, body language, facial expressions, clothing choices, intensity, and, of course, your words, all speak volumes to the team.

Is there a "proper" style for a sales manager? I can't say there is. Do we all need to act like impassioned football coaches or have the leadership ability of Vince Lombardi to create a winning sales culture? No we don't. I've seen men and women with varying personality styles and approaches do very nice jobs leading their sales teams. But if you allow me to editorialize a bit, I do believe there is something to be gleaned from professional sports coaches, particularly because sports coaches are judged by wins and losses (results) just like sales managers are!

I'm a huge American football fan. Several times per year I find occasion to turn something I observe during football season into a blog post for the sales community. It's easy to make analogies between athletes and salespeople, coaches and sales managers, or sports teams and sales teams. As someone who observes and consults business leaders for a living, I pay particular attention to high-profile football coaches.

Over the past several years I have been absolutely intrigued by Jim Harbaugh, who at the time I'm writing this is just a few months into his tenure as the head football coach at the prestigious University of Michigan. Michigan has a long, proud tradition of winning but has suffered mightily over the past decade with losing season after losing season. Harbaugh, who has become known as a turnaround specialist, and who also happens to be a Michigan alum, was hired to restore glory to his alma mater's football program.

Harbaugh has an impressive track record for turning around teams. He took over as coach of the practically unknown University of San Diego football program and led the team to two Division I-AA championships in three years. He then left for Stanford University, where he inherited a team that had just completed a 1-11 season. That's right, one win and eleven losses. Just a few years later they finished with a 12-1 record and ranked Number 4 in the nation. Harbaugh moved on to try his hand at coaching an NFL team and took the reins of the San Francisco 49ers as they were coming off an abysmal 6-10 season. Would you like to guess what he helped accomplish there? How about three straight trips to the NFC Championship Game and one Super Bowl appearance!

You don't need to be a consultant or a football fan to understand that Harbaugh knows a thing or two about winning and that he probably has a pretty darn good handle on leadership and culture. So I tuned in to the University of Michigan press conference introducing Harbaugh as the new coach, hoping to glean a leadership nugget or two. Harbaugh did not disappoint. After making some first-class, heartfelt, and very appropriate comments, Harbaugh took questions from the throng of reporters. One reporter prefaced his question by mentioning the success Harbaugh had turning around organizations and then asked how he would get Michigan football winning again. The room fell silent as Harbaugh paused before answering. He then provided this powerful response that all of us in business, particularly in sales leadership, should take to heart:

"We are going to start winning at our first team meeting."

I was struck by the simplicity and the clarity of his answer. It took all of two seconds to for him to articulate, yet I could not get it out of my head for days.

What would it look like for you to help your team start winning at your next sales meeting? How might your tone, approach, and expectations have to change?

Let me be direct here. As the sales leader, you must be positive and optimistic. It's your job to point to the sales goal and tell the troops that *we are going to hit it; we are going to win!* Yes, earlier I did say that various personality types can succeed in sales management roles. Not everyone needs to be a wildly extroverted cheerleader, and in certain businesses a more reserved person might even be a better fit. But there is one trait that sales managers absolutely cannot have: negativity. If the manager is negative, the team is doomed. Going back to the leadership truths shared in Chapter 1: As goes the leader, so goes the team. The level of the team rarely, if ever, exceeds the level of the leader. If the leader doesn't have a winning attitude, there is no way the team will.

As you gather your team for meetings, what message are you sending? Everyone is looking to you to set the tone and the pace.

Look over your recent sales meeting agendas. Which regular agenda items have become stale or useless and should be deleted? What potential agenda topics deserve more time and would help you not only alter the dynamic in the meeting, but also foster the kind of winning culture you want to establish? How are you challenging the team, engaging their hearts, and helping each salesperson to see himself as part of something great?

Take advantage of this wonderful platform to lead, influence, and equip your team. The sales team meeting shouldn't be seen as drudgery or something you take for granted and do by rote.

Here's one last idea if you're serious about ramping up team meetings. Call together a few of your best people and ask them for honest feedback about past sales meetings. Solicit their input for what they'd like to see and ask what would be most valuable to them. I guarantee that you will get very useful information, and your people will appreciate that you sought their input. It's worth repeating: Salespeople should look forward to team meetings because they benefit from being there and leave more energized and better equipped to win.

CHAPTER 22

Sales Managers Must Get Out in the Field with Salespeople

It sure seems like "fieldwork"—going out in the field to work along-side salespeople—has become a lost art.

Before going any further, let me quickly address those who lead inside sales teams so they don't feel slighted or annoyed by my use of the term *fieldwork*. Inside sales teams continue to grow in popularity. I have consulted for and coached a number of exclusively inside sales teams over the past few years and have tremendous respect for them and their managers. Inside sales is real sales—a full sales job. By field-work, I am simply referring to the act of working alongside a salesper-son as she does her job.

The same truths and principles presented in this chapter absolutely apply to both inside and outside sales managers. Of course, you don't get the "windshield time" to talk life and sales with an inside salesperson as you do with someone who manages outside salespeople, but my hope is that after reading this chapter you will be convinced of the need to spend more time in and out of the office with team members.

My colleagues in the sales improvement business give me a funny look when they discover that I will occasionally fly to a salesperson's market and jump in their car to spend a full day in the field observing and coaching. I didn't realize how few consultants, speakers, and coaches head out to work in the field. I don't do it as much as I'd like to, but I still love to get out there whenever possible. I probably learn ten times more about the business and the sales talent in the field than in the office. When working with a salesperson, I'm fond of saying that every day out in the field selling is better than any day in the office. That's where sales happens!

You Can't Lead a Sales Attack from Behind Your Desk

I'm sorry, but you are not commanding pilots of unmanned aerial vehicles (UAVs, drones) who sit in bunkers flying aircraft on missions thousands of miles away. Air Force commanders are able to evaluate and coach UAV pilots by observing their work on a monitor, but you cannot manage salespeople, whose primary job is to interact with other people, by staring into your CRM screen. A CRM screen does not permit you to see, feel, and hear how your people do their most important job. Let me repeat one more time that you manage people whose primary job is to interact with other people! It's not possible to properly lead your troops by working solely from your ivory tower.

When visiting a client's office, I like to wander around the sales department to get a sense of the interaction and activity. If it's an inside sales team, I get concerned when there are really long periods where a salesperson isn't making outbound calls or proactively emailing customers and prospects. Similarly, I scratch my head when the majority of people on an *outside* team are sitting around *inside* the office. I like to tease the reps in an inquisitive tone. "What are you doing here? There are no customers or prospects in the office." Frankly, that same question needs to be asked more often to the managers of these teams, who should be out working alongside their people and meeting with important clients. Listen, I get that you have other responsibilities, that there's *work* to be done and internal meetings to attend. But the cold hard truth is that to do your job effectively, a significant portion of your time must be spent in the field, where business is conducted.

Let me be even more direct with this exhortation. Fieldwork is not just another activity that would be "nice to do." Or, as some managers explain when asked why they spend so little time out working with members of their team, "I'd like to, but I just can't get to it. There is too much else on my plate." Hear me clearly: This is a "have to" not an "I'd like to get to it someday" task. Fieldwork *is* your job. It's not optional. This isn't like trying to decide if you want the push-button start and heated seats when buying a car. This is the transmission! No transmission = no car.

Powerful Benefits Accrue to the Sales Manager Who Gets Out in the Field

Working with your people is one of the highest-value uses of your time because it pays huge dividends to you as the leader, to the salesperson, and to the business. Each of the following benefits, in and of themselves, would be worth your time and attention, but you usually can accomplish all five every time you're out in the field.

1. Riding along with your salespeople provides the opportunity to observe them in action. There is no substitute for watching and listening to your people prepare for and conduct sales calls. And that's just the beginning of what we're looking for when traveling with and evaluating them. Beyond getting to see how they handle customers and how the customers respond, it helps you get a feel for how they plan their days and handle other aspects of the job.

You also need to pay attention to the *professional* and more intangible aspects of being in sales. Is the car clean? Is your salesperson dressed appropriately? Does she know her way around the territory or town she's supposedly working? Is she prepared? Does she show up on time? When a rep dresses poorly or bombs conducting a sales call in front of me, I wonder if this is her best effort when she's trying to impress an important guest, what must she be like when no one is watching?

When you hop in a salesperson's car that feels like a pigsty or find him wearing a threadbare company logo shirt that should have been retired about thirty washes ago, it's hard to view that person as a professional who represents his company well. I once headed out to work with a salesperson who was on the bubble. The president and I put a giant question mark on this guy's chest and were working to figure out if he was going to make it. I flew into a city where he was already working. The plan was for the rep to pick me up curbside at the airport. He arrived twenty minutes late, leaving me standing out in the cold waiting for him. That's what known as a CLM, a career-limiting move. Again, the natural questions: How often do you keep customers waiting if you show up twenty minutes late to pick up a VIP visitor? Do you have trouble managing your time on a daily basis? How screwed up are your priorities? FYI, that salesperson did not survive at the company much longer.

2. Working in the field presents a priceless opportunity to coach your salesperson before and after sales calls. Earlier I mentioned how much I benefited from sales managers riding with me early in my career. I am forever indebted to those guys. What took place twenty-five years ago I remember like it was yesterday. Often, we'd do pre-call planning before leaving the office, or at the hotel if out of town. Even so, when I'd pull into the customer's parking lot, I can recall reaching to turn off the ignition only to have my manager reach out to stop me, "Not so fast. Leave the car on; I need the air conditioning. Let's go over this one more time. Remind me of the names and personalities of the people with whom we're meeting. And what are their expectations for the meeting? Tell me what's a win for us coming out of here today? What's your plan for the call and what are the biggest challenges we'll face?"

The coaching continued during the debrief following the meeting. One of the lessons I picked up from a mentor was to always let the salesperson share her take on the meeting first. Instead of jumping right in and providing feedback, ask her how she thought it went. Once we're back in the car, I'll prompt the salesperson with simple questions like, "How'd we do?" or "Well, what do you think?" I want to hear the rep's assessment so I can compare it to mine. Sometimes it helps to lead a bit: "What did you do well, and what might you have done differently?

Once I've pulled as much information as possible from the salesperson, I'll share my observations. Being the third person in the room is one of my absolute favorite things to do; it's amazing how much you can absorb when you're not burdened with conducting the call, but just observing. I take tons of notes during sales calls. It looks great, because the customer and salesperson both think I'm making business notes about the customer's issues or the opportunities we're uncovering. That's far from the case. I'm writing down observations about the salesperson, the interaction, specific things that were said (or should have been), and more. I even track the percentage of time the salesperson talks against the amount the buyer talks. Salespeople are often horrified when I inform them they spent 80 percent of the meeting talking. As one of my mentors liked to say, "You did a nice job presenting, but you talked too much. When you're talking, you're not learning." That particular mentor is worth over $2 billion today, so maybe we should heed his advice!

Even sales managers who wouldn't be considered sales gurus can share helpful observations with their people. You don't have to be a sales trainer or author to provide honest feedback on how the salesperson built rapport, shared her agenda, positioned the company, asked probing questions, presented a potential solution, and attempted to flesh out potential obstacles, objections, and next steps.

Coaching in the field is invaluable. Some may argue that managers can debrief a salesperson without having been along for the meeting. Sure they can. But they'd have only one perspective. Can you really coach a salesperson based solely on what that person shares with you from his own perspective? Of course not. Would you want your golf instructor to coach your swing based on how you told him you were playing, or might it make more sense for him to actually see you in action before offering suggestions?

3. Windshield time and mealtime provide a rare opportunity to learn more about your salespeople and make you a more effective manager. As much as I love the whole coaching dynamic surrounding making sales calls with salespeople, some of the most valuable time comes when we are not discussing business. Truly good managers get to know their people on a deeper level. No, I'm not advocating personal friendships between managers and their team members. There are obviously inherent dangers with that, although I'd admit that friendships are often formed and that they can be more positive than negative. But friendship is not the goal. The main objective is to get to know what makes each of your people tick so you can best help them succeed. Your job as the manager is to win by helping your people win. If you can help a salesperson win, you will be not only admired and respected, you'll be considered a great leader—and a leader for whom that salesperson will run through, around, and over walls!

You do not need to talk business 100 percent of the time you're with a salesperson. It would be weird if you did. If you showed no care or concern for the human being behind the salesperson, what would that communicate to your team members? Nobody wants to go the extra mile or put out a supreme effort for a robotic manager. This is sales, right? We've already looked at how heart-engagement is critical. So take advantage of a full day (or days) with someone to engage in personal dialogue. When driving from place to place or sitting together over a meal, swap stories. Ask penetrating questions. Show interest. Find out what's important to this person. It may sound trite, but these things matter. If you discover your salesperson loves a certain sports team or NASCAR driver, make a mental note of it. Then when you see that team or driver make the news, shoot a quick text message to the rep. It shows that you listen, that you actually have the person on your mind, and that you care about more than her sales numbers.

4. Getting out of the office provides you with a firsthand look at what is taking place in the market. The truth is that sometimes you just need to see and hear things with your own eyes and ears. One of the biggest complaints salespeople make about their company's senior leaders is that they're clueless about what's going on in the trenches. As mentioned earlier, most salespeople have no trouble speaking up to bitch about policies, product, programs, or pricing that make no sense. The problem is that because they are known for doing this, and for exaggerating how *tough* it is, their pleas often fall on deaf ears or are simply viewed as excuses. That's why it's imperative that frontline sales managers and senior executives get out in the field with salespeople so they can get a read on reality in the marketplace.

Back in 2009, I was leading a sales team selling marketing services. Advertising agencies were one of our core customer segments. Their businesses were being devastated by the lethal combination of the pullback caused by the real estate/financial market collapse in late 2008 and the social media revolution hitting at the same time. Not only were marketing expenditures slashed to preserve cash during the downturn, but marketing executives were challenged as to whether traditional print, mail, and fulfillment were even needed since this new social media thing was free. It was an unmitigated disaster. In my twenty-five years in business, I'd never experienced such futility in a sales initiative.

My team had good talent, a good plan, a good story, and a strategic target account list along with my best effort and coaching. But selling into that market segment at that time in history was as fruitless as banging our heads against a wall. It became very clear to me that our company did not have a sales problem; we had a strategy problem. The market we served was undergoing transformational shift, and no amount of cajoling, rewarding, or threatening was going to change the reality that we were not going to hit our goals selling into that headwind.

Our executive committee was filled with bright people, many of whom had been in this industry for three decades. They were having a hard time coming to grips with the news my team and I were bringing back from the field. So I grabbed a few days on our CEO's calendar and insisted he join me on a trip to several key cities in North Carolina, where I was spending significant energy. He was happy to join me. Taking advantage of the fact I'd have the big guy in tow, I was able to secure meetings with several top people, including a few owners, at agencies across the state. Needless to say, the trip served its purpose. Upon returning to the office, the CEO gathered the executive committee, shared what he personally observed in the field, and began plans to revise a portion of the company's strategy.

When you go out in the field, you get a dose of reality. About ten years ago, I was doing a project for the COO of a $100 million company that sent me into several of its markets over the course of a month. That company's new sales executive was in the process of undertaking a significant reorganization and also having the sales team focus aggressively on selling a particular segment of the company's product offering. It happened to be a segment of the business that he liked and believed there was significant opportunity to grow.

After making a few dozen sales calls with three different regional salespeople during that month, it was patently obvious that this guy likely gathered his market intelligence while in the men's room or by taking advice from taxi drivers. I'm no strategist, just a sales hunter turned consultant, but you'd have to be blind and deaf to not conclude what I did from those thirty-plus sales calls. There was zero potential for growing the segment of the business on which the sales leader was focusing the sales team. It wasn't even that customers were not interested in the company's offerings. It was that this customer segment was dying! These reps took me into dying account after dying account. I could just about smell the stench of death. I brought my findings back to the COO, who quickly intervened. That sales leader was sending his troops on a kamikaze mission based on a gut feeling and personal preference. There is no way in the world he would've committed to that strategy if he had spent the time in the market that I had. No way.

It bears repeating: It is very dangerous attempting to lead a sales effort from your ivory tower.

5. Fieldwork helps you develop important relationships with key customers. This fifth benefit of getting out with your people may be the most compelling of all. Getting face-to-face with your company's largest, most growable, and most at-risk accounts can pay huge dividends. When a sales manager or executive visits with customers, the dynamic in the room changes. The leader brings a gravitas representing the company alongside the regular salesperson. Your presence not only communicates to the customers that they're important, it also tends to elevate the conversation beyond the typical buyer-seller exchange.

The truth is that executives and managers are perceived and treated differently from the salesperson. Some of that is attributable to the way we carry ourselves and the approach we take. But honestly, much of it is simply due to the title. Wearing the mantle of sales manager carries certain benefits. Customers see you as an authority and tend to be willing to discuss higher-level issues.

There is both a strong offensive and defensive rationale for the sales leader to build relationships with key customers. From an offensive posture, your involvement often creates access to more senior people within the customer organization. It's just logical that when you show up, there is a better probability of securing time with higher-level executives. And from a defensive posture, maintaining relationships with key customer contacts can be crucial should the salesperson fall out of favor with the account or leave your company. When you have a relationship with the customer, the transition is much smoother and much less risky than if you're an unknown commodity.

When with Your Salesperson, Be Present with Your Salesperson

This should go without saying, but in today's hyper-connected, smart-phone-addicted world, it truly does need to be said. Just admit it: You're addicted. And if you're a sales manager, you're likely double addicted!

These are new challenges of the past decade. Back in the "old days" when I was selling and my manager or an executive would join me in the field, when they were with me—they were with me. If my manager was in the passenger seat of my car, or a rental car, he didn't have his head down thumb-scrolling through his email or Twitter feed. In fact, if we go way back to my early career, neither my boss nor I even had a phone, let alone email and the Internet.

Brace yourselves, young people. You know what we did a couple of times a day to keep up with our messages and respond to a customer's request? (Key phrase: a couple of times a day.) We'd find a bank of payphones, hopefully just off the lobby in an upscale hotel. The manager would grab one phone and I'd grab another. We'd each call into a central voice-mail system to retrieve our messages. There would be a handful of items requiring a response but nothing like the dozens and dozens of emails our own company and customers send us today. And invariably, by the time I got through my messages, there would be one more new message that wasn't there initially. This one would be from the sales manager, of course. He would hear something in a message that required distribution to the sales team. Or even better, he'd forward a success story message that another salesperson left for him. Oh, those were the days!

After checking our messages, we'd agree that we each needed about ten minutes to return a couple of calls. When we were done, we'd jump back in the car. Why do I tell this story? I share it because there are some very practical lessons about productivity and courtesy, and how we used to respect each other's time. When my manager was with me, he was with me. He wasn't participating on corporate conference calls while we were driving to see an account. He wasn't pre-occupied reading and answering emails sent to him *all day long* by other sales team members and various people inside the company. Nope. For the majority of the day, I was his focus.

Sales managers, can I suggest we resurrect a page from an old playbook? Instead of constantly dealing with emails and messages when you're in the field with a salesperson, what if you agreed to take a couple of set breaks during the day so each of you could respond to matters requiring your attention? You don't need a bank of payphones anymore, but you can easily call a twenty-minute Starbucks timeout to return a call and catch up on emails. Then, when you reconnect with your salesperson, try something novel: Turn your phone off. Not vibrate. Not "do not disturb." Off off.

Please allow me to challenge you with this thought: If as a sales manager or executive you can't go two or three hours without looking at your email or returning a phone call, then something is fundamentally dysfunctional with how you are doing your job and/or what your company expects of you. Feel free to quote me on that to your private equity group owner or crazed CEO who thinks you exist to answer his every fleeting question the moment he has one.

Do you remember how we used to poke fun at people who carried beepers? Well, today we all have beepers, except they do much more than just beep or buzz, and they have iPhone or BlackBerry engraved on the case! Please hear me: You are not a freaking heart surgeon or the assistant to the president of the United States charged with carrying around the nuclear "football" with the missile launch codes. No one is going to die waiting a couple of hours for a response from you. I know that making yourself unavailable for a short period of time to focus on a high-value activity is a radical thought in today's business world. But like our parents taught us, just because *everyone else* is doing something, doesn't make it right. And just because technology enables people to reach you 24/7, that doesn't mean it's a good idea. Respect your team members by showing them they are your priority when you're with them in the field.

Don't Do Your Salesperson's Job

By all means, you should actively participate in meetings with clients and prospects. And when you're mentoring people on how sales calls should be conducted, whether they are new or simply need to improve, it is absolutely fine to model for them how you would like to see it done. In other words, it makes sense to demonstrate good sales technique for people you are coaching. But that should be the exception, not the rule. For the most part, you go in the field to observe and coach, not to do the salespeople's jobs for them. In Chapter 6, I was critical of the sales manager with a hero complex who continually feels the need to jump in and take over on sales calls. Be especially alert for this behavior if you have that tendency.

Listen, everyone understands if once in a while you have to toss your salesperson a life preserver because he's drowning in front of an important customer. Feel free to rescue your person and save the deal, too. But if you find yourself doing that more often than not, then you're the problem, not the salesperson. Plus, we all know that painful failures create powerful learning opportunities. So, while I'm all for maximizing sales and saving most opportunities, there can more be long-term benefit by letting your salespeople suffer through their own mistakes and the agony of defeat. After a good flop, people tend to be more open to coaching.

The best coaches model the way and then get out of the way. You're the coach and the manager, not the player. Don't do your salespeople's jobs for them. That is not a reproducible model. This hackneyed proverb really does apply here. "Give a man a fish and you feed him for a day; teach a man to fish and you feed him for a lifetime." Leverage your personal sales prowess by building it into your people. As one sales leader, you cannot possibly cover the whole world.

Go *with* Your People, and Go with Them Often

I have two concluding exhortations about your work in the field. It's surprising this first one is even necessary. When you go in the field, go with a salesperson. I know, that sounds obvious. But I'm aware of several cases where sales managers headed out to see a salesperson's account without her. There are rare occasions when that might make sense. If a big customer complained about the salesperson, I could see why we'd go learn more without the salesperson present. And at times there are meetings for "executives only."

In the situations I discovered recently, that was not the case. At one company, management did not like the salesperson and was on a mission to discredit him. Various executives would intentionally interact with the customer. It was an underhanded way of rationalizing their refusal to give credit to the salesperson for the success he was having. I've seen other companies' management meet with a customer and then not update the salesperson on what took place. That creates mistrust and often diminishes the salesperson in the customer's eyes because it looks like she's in the dark. If you have an issue with a salesperson, deal with it like an adult. Confront it head on. Don't do the passive-aggressive thing or play games. No one wins that way, and you risk creating mistrust across the entire sales organization.

Other cases of the sales manager flying solo are more innocent. Sometimes it is just a matter of speed or convenience. The manager badly wants to see a particular market or customer and makes his own plans irrespective of the salesperson's availability. The manager's intentions may be good, but the consequences to the manager-salesperson relationship usually are not. My bottom line is this: If you are the full-time manager or executive over sales, and you are not the day-to-day owner of the customer relationship, unless it's one of those special occasions mentioned previously, it's hard to make the case that you should be calling on the customer without the salesperson. Every time you do, you're missing an opportunity to mentor and influence your salesperson. Plus, you run the risk of damaging her trust in you and taking wind out of her sails.

The final encouragement is regarding how frequently you should get out in the field. There is no one "right" answer to that question. It depends on a lot of factors, including the size of your team, how much support you have in the office, and, of course, how much other non-sales crap you or your company piles on your desk.

I'm convinced that your three highest-value, highest-payoff activities as the sales leader are meeting 1:1 with your people, leading productive sales team meetings, and working in the field *alongside* members of the team. This I can share: Of the approximately 150 companies I've worked with, only twice have I been concerned that a sales leader was spending too much time away from the office, out in the field. Both of those managers were literally traveling upwards of 90 percent of the time. They were constantly on the run. One guy was attempting to play Superman and singlehandedly grow the business across the entire United States. And the other guy appeared to be on the run from his home life and his administrative responsibilities back in the office.

I'm all for field work, but the other two high-value activities plus corporate responsibilities require your focus as well. I hesitate to toss out a number for how often a manager should be out in the field. Different businesses place different types of burdens on the sales leader. However, I am very comfortable declaring that in almost every case, the manager could stand to get of the office more often. In some businesses, that might mean being in the field two-thirds of the time; in others, one-third might seem a high bar to set. For a true sales leader, every day of fieldwork is better than any day in the office.

If you are serious about leading your sales team and establishing a winning, high-performance culture, talk constantly about goals and results, and get with your salespeople 1:1, in team meetings, and in the field.

CHAPTER 23

Talent Management Can Make or Break the Sales Leader

Talent changes everything. The right talent can make your life a joy; talent deficiencies can make your life miserable and destroy your sales effort. It's that big a deal. Next to leading your team well and building a healthy culture, talent management is the most critical aspect of the sales manager's job.

Some sales experts would make a strong argument that talent trumps all other factors. They say that the right talent finds a way to win regardless of circumstances. My only disagreement with that assertion is that poor leadership and an unhealthy culture will eventually overcome even the strongest people, and over time cause top producers to pack their bags and take their talents elsewhere. Nonetheless, talent is the second essential element of the sales leadership framework, and without it, you have almost no chance to win at the game of sales.

My New York sales executive father used a helpful metaphor when stressing the importance of sales talent to regional and district managers around the country. He'd say that it's not the power of the electric company that lights the room, it's the wattage of the bulb. I was probably a teenager when I first heard him say that. And it stuck. My dad's point was that it didn't matter how powerful the company brand or how brilliant the corporate sales plan if you didn't have the appropriate talent in the field facing the customer. You can send an enormous jolt of electric juice down the power line, but it's all for naught if the bulb in the room you're trying to light is short on watts.

On that note, let's shed some light on sales talent management by diving into the Four Rs first mentioned in Chapter 17:

1. Right People in the Right Roles

2. Retain Top Producers

3. Remediate or Replace Underperformers (Coach up or coach out)

4. Recruit

Get the Right People in the Right Roles

Getting the right people in the right roles is your first and most challenging talent priority. Those eight words may be simple to say, but you will encounter two significant hurdles attempting to accomplish that task.

1. There is a shortage of solid sales talent.

2. Most companies lack the desire, insight, and patience to properly define sales roles.

It's a widely accepted reality that there are not enough good salespeople to go around. If you doubt me, try to find an unemployed A-player salesperson. You won't; they don't exist. I won't quote empirical data because I'm not a big proponent of most sales studies and statistics. There is often a fair amount of chicanery to produce the study's desired outcome. Isn't it amazing how supposedly *unbiased* studies by "experts" in the sales improvement profession seem to magically point people to serious problems for which these experts have the perfect remedy? Call me a skeptic, but I've learned to be wary of studies and statistics quoted by purported experts.

However, I am not wary of what I'm able to see with my own eyes. In the companies I'm in and around, true A-players, consistent top producers, make up between 10 and 20 percent of the sales population. A company stacked with talent might have one-fourth A-players, while one short on top talent might operate with only one-tenth labeled as an A. This shortage of top talent is why it is imperative to maximize the impact of your A-players, and ensure that they're happy and intent on staying with your company. We'll circle back to look at practical ways to retain top producers in just a moment.

A lean talent pool forces us to become smarter talent managers. Here are three practical ways to increase your talent IQ and catalyze getting the right people in the right jobs.

1. Do away with the naive deployment philosophy that there is one catch-all generic sales job. I began this conversation in Chapter 8 by intentionally listing a wide variety of sales roles early. Believing that a sales job is a sales job is as foolish as declaring that a doctor is a doctor. Would you want to see a proctologist for a problem with your feet, or a podiatrist to resolve an issue in that awkward place the proctologist works? Didn't think so. So why do the majority of companies settle for a one-size-fits-all sales role?

I challenge you to step back and look at the job description you use for the basic sales position in your company. Read that description and ponder the natural talents and acquired skills necessary to do all phases of that job well. Then chart out the phases of your sales process from Genesis to Revelation. I mean it. Write down every phase of what's expected of the typical salesperson from the earliest stage of trying to get a prospect's attention and secure a meeting; through the middle stages of conducting discovery sales calls, probing, building consensus, and presenting; to the latter stages of proposing, negotiating, and closing. Don't forget to include what you expect your jack-of-all-trades "salesperson" to do after the sale, which for many businesses includes onboarding new clients, serving as the main contact, maintaining key relationships, quoting additional work, entertaining, cross-selling new offerings, and, of course, fighting customer service fires and providing Mach 1 response time to the customer's every request. I'm out of breath just from reading that list of responsibilities!

My hope is that relooking at the job description and the overwhelming list of expected duties causes you to pause. Are these realistic expectations of what one human being can do? Just out of curiosity, may I ask if there is even one other position in your entire organization tasked with such a wide range of responsibilities? My guess is that there is not. Need I even bring up that this isn't any old position we are talking about here—this is the sales position, the one you and every employee are counting on to bring in the new customers and new revenue that are the lifeblood of any business.

Beyond just the "capacity" issue that I'm begging you to reconsider, there is a bigger impediment to success that deserves even more of your attention. Reality is that it would require a uniquely talented and extremely versatile individual, a super human, to be competent at everything most companies ask their generic salesperson to do. Sales results suffer because we spread salespeople too thin, and even more so because almost no one is good at both extreme ends of the sales spectrum: prospecting and hunting on the front end and account management and maintenance on the back end.

2. Stop pretending that zookeepers will be successful hunters. There may not be a wider sales talent management blind spot than this one. We're all familiar with the standard hunter-farmer sales role conundrum, yet so few companies demonstrate the patience and desire to further define sales roles. The hybrid hunter-farmer role dominates most business-to-business sales organizations today. One guy or gal does it all: create, open, and close deals, and then manage the customer relationship. It's the default model. Everyone uses it. Why bother creating more work for ourselves to create something different? I'll tell you why: because the model sucks. Putting it more diplomatically, it's suboptimal. It's not the best of both worlds; it's the worst. And it's absolutely killing your sales team's ability to develop new business for two irrefutable reasons.

The first reason has to do with the hard-wiring, preferences, and comfort zones of today's prototypical account manager salesperson. The majority of the sales population has the DNA of an account manager. They're highly relational and likable, and the really good ones are also service oriented and reliable. People like this often thrive in sales roles when there's plenty of incoming demand and business to manage. If they've been around an industry or company long enough, they also benefit from becoming product or technical experts. For the most part, everyone, including the customer, loves these kinds of salespeople. But, and this is a big but, account managers tend to be productive only when they're fed work or servicing existing customers. They excel at *managing* accounts, but not at creating them.

A few years ago I led a full-day session for the management team of a company whose business was off badly. They had very tenured salespeople who *managed* large geographic territories. We got into a discussion about sales talent, and I asked each sales manager to grade each of his people. One of the older gentlemen in the room was quick to chime in, "I know our problem. Some salespeople are bird hunters and some are big-game hunters, and we have too many bird hunters." People in the room nodded in affirmation and a few made comments. I stood there for a minute, and then retorted with, "*Sure, some of your people are small-game hunters and not enough go after the big kill, but isn't the real problem that most of the folks on your teams are zookeepers?*"

The zookeeper analogy came out of thin air. I hadn't used that expression before. I continue to use it years later because it's more accurate and creates more contrast than the standard hunter versus farmer comparison. Think about the highly relational, nurturing people on your sales team while picturing a zookeeper cuddling with and feeding a bottle to a cute little baby mammal. While these are wonderful people who do an outstanding job caring for and protecting those under their charge, what in the world makes us think they would ever pick up a weapon and head out on a hunt? That's never going to happen. Never ever. Think about the absurdity of asking a zookeeper to trade the animal baby bottle for a weapon. Isn't it safe to assume that someone who liked to hunt wouldn't have a job as a zookeeper, and vice versa? So why are we surprised that account manager–type salespeople, who typically dislike conflict, risk, and rejection (standard fare for the sales hunter), are often reluctant to prospect or pursue new business, or fail at it when they do? It's past time to stop hoping and pretending that our zookeepers will become successful new business developers.

3. Free up your excellent sales hunters so they can maximize their time hunting. Even more perplexing than management asking zookeepers and farmers to hunt is that most companies require their best hunters to spend an inordinate amount of time on nonhunting activities. This makes me crazy because it is crazy.

Who decided this was a good idea? Companies that are hurting for new business and are short on true sales hunters burden the precious few they have with excessive nonhunting responsibilities. It's the absolute dumbest thing I see in sales. Okay, maybe the second dumbest next to paying salespeople the same commission rate to babysit accounts that were sold ten years ago as they earn for acquiring new accounts.

Why would we ever consider taking someone away from a highly important task at which they excel, something that we badly need (new business development), to put them on lower-value tasks that many others are more capable of doing and more willing to do? Even more maddening is that I rarely get pushback about this assertion. Executives agree with the premise that sales hunters should be freed up to hunt. Yet most refuse to better define their company's sales roles or do the hard work of revamping how their sales force operates.

Making this as plain as possible, most organizations have an over-abundance of account manager/farmer/zookeeper salespeople and a dire shortage of true sales killers/rainmakers/hunters. In order to maximize the impact of your hunters, maximize the amount of time they get to spend hunting. And the best way to do this is to strip as much account management and service responsibility away from them as possible.

The company I worked for back in the late 1990s, the one with the "sales heaven" culture, took advantage of this idea, and I was the beneficiary. A very successful salesperson at this company sold and managed between $1.5 million and $2.5 million per year. There were several talented, driven producers consistently booking that much business and making a great living from it. But they were effectively capped at that range because so much of their time and focus went to servicing and reselling projects to their existing clients.

During my second year there, I began having significant success picking up new clients. Company leadership recognized my penchant for prospecting and big-game hunting, while also perceiving that I wasn't the best project manager and maintenance guy. Imagine that, a top sales hunter not so good at details and service work! Unlike at many organizations, these leaders were willing to do the work to tin-ker with the sales model to maximize the impact I could have on the business. The decision was made that I would no longer *manage* accounts that I acquired. Sure, I'd stay in touch with key client con-tacts and keep my eyes and ears open looking for new opportunities within the account, but the bulk of the day-to-day account manage-ment and project coordination was taken away from me. The com-pany surrounded me with a team of highly competent account managers and made it crystal clear that my primary job was to go out and slay new business while leaving the account management to my teammates. Our newly created team sold over $7 million my third year with the company—about triple what the typical good sales team produced. Why? Because the company put the right people in the right sales roles. Everyone was happy. Everyone won—the hunter, the account managers, the clients, and the company.

Make Darn Sure to Retain Your Best Salespeople

Almost nothing hurts a sales leader as much as losing a top producer, especially because they are almost impossible to replace. Next to ensuring that you have the right people in the right roles, Job #1 is keeping your best people on your team and fully engaged. Here's a simple list worth running through every so often:

- ► Who are your very best people who would devastate you if they left?

- ► How happy are they?

- ► How do you know they're as happy as you think they are?

- ► What are you personally doing to communicate their importance to you?

- ► What are other key executives doing to demonstrate appreciation for these stars?

- ► In what ways are you demonstrably working to make their work lives easier and put them in a position to even further maximize their results?

Do not take for granted that your top people are happy because they're on top of the sales rankings. Smack yourself any time you start thinking that they wouldn't leave because they're making too much money. That's a silly thought. Top salespeople are typically the most driven people on your team—driven to win, driven to sell, driven to earn. That's also why they can be rather demanding or high mainte-nance. Speaking from experience (mine and others), your top producers can actually be the first to jump ship when incredibly frustrated or if they sense something fundamentally wrong at the company that could reduce their chance of winning in the future. Just like we see professional athletes leave teams where they are the beloved star to join a championship contender, competitive salespeople want to play for a winning team.

One of the most valuable things you can do is learn what makes each of your A-players tick. Don't assume it's public recognition just because that's a stereotype. I have coached quite a few private, introverted sales killers who couldn't stand getting called up in front of the company or being praised constantly in public. Take the time to truly understand what drives each individual. The answers may surprise you. For some, it's freedom. Others want their voice heard and a say in big decisions. Some want the trophy and tangible prize (like the Masters champion Green Jacket) so the whole world knows they are the top dog. Personally, when I was selling, I didn't care much for the public praise. Just being listed at the top of the sales report was recognition enough. What really kept my heart engaged were private meetings with the senior executives or company owners. I deeply wanted two things: to be appreciated and to be heard. Tell me privately how much my personal contribution means to you and the company and my heart leaps. Listen to my thoughts on dumb corporate policies, needed sales tools, or sales compensation, and I'll sell my ass off, and put on the corporate underwear telling every employee how great the company is.

Do not ignore your best people. I know many will think that's an odd, unnecessary proclamation, but it's very common for managers, particularly inexperienced ones, to forget about their top performers. Most managers have too much on their plate and their hands full. They're buried in corporate crap and administrative work. When feeling pressure to make numbers, they naturally (and wrongly) focus on their underperformers.

It's so easy for a manager to think to himself about a top producer, "She's doing great and blowing her numbers out of the water.

I can forget about her in order to deal with my problem children." That is awfully flawed reasoning on multiple levels. First, there's the retention issue we've been reviewing. Beyond that, though, is a management philosophy that does not get enough attention: In many cases, it is your best people who have the best chance to grow the business. If you need more sales, who is best suited and most like to go get them? Your top producers, that's who!

My father was always preaching that managers make the mistake of overinvesting in their worst performers at the expense of their best people. He would make the case that your top people deserve more, not less, of your attention and focus because they're the ones who know what to do with it. Want to keep your best people super-happy and drive more sales as quickly as possible? Over-support your A-players, clear the decks to remove obstacles in their way, and focus them like lasers on the biggest and best new markets and opportunities. This seems like the appropriate place to offer a gentle reminder: The job of the sales manager is not to manage the sales department. Your primary job is to drive sales. There is no extra credit for dividing your time equally across all of your people, but there is fame and fortune for the sales leader who consistently over-delivers on results.

Set aside specific time blocks in your calendar for the sole purpose of investing in your A-players. Find creative ways to show them they're loved. Think outside the box. Maybe you create a Top Dog Retreat for a few of your very best. Take a trip with a handful of senior executives and the Top Dogs. Spend half of the retreat playing and treating these salespeople like royalty. Use the other half for serious meetings to get their input on a variety of topics and also have them ask management the hard questions. Can you imagine how pumped and loyal top producers would be following that kind of experience?

Nothing hurts worse than losing a top-producing salesperson. Smart sales talent management dictates that you invest the time and creativity to retain your best folks.

Remediate or Replace: Coach Up or Coach Out Underperformers

While I am advocating that managers invest more time with top performers, in no way does that imply they should ignore underperformance. Too often, sales managers let underperformance go for too long before addressing it head-on. Sales is about results; it is not about being busy, productive, or a good corporate citizen. Sales team leaders are judged by the results their teams deliver, not by how nice team members are or how hard they work. The manager has no choice but to address those on his team whose results fall short of expectations.

Sales managers tend to fall into two extreme camps when it comes to dealing with laggards. On one hand are those that are quick to cut and run. They have an anxious trigger finger, and at the first sign of weakness they'll send someone packing. Then there are the overly patient managers who avoid hard conversations at all cost, or the extremely optimistic types who perpetually hope their underperformers are just about to turn it around.

I believe there's a better way—a happy medium—that would help managers in both camps become more effective talent managers. For lack of a better term, I simply call it remediation. Remediation has two stages, informal and formal, and one goal: to coach up or coach out those whose results are not acceptable. Informal remediation comes first. It's when we let a salesperson know that his performance is unacceptable and we are going to work *with* him to address it. Formal remediation would follow if results did not improve, and it's typically nothing more than the *formal* process for removing a team member.

The beautiful thing about a well-executed remediation is that it always works. Both possible outcomes are good for the company, the manager, and even the struggling salesperson. Either the underperformer improves to a level that's acceptable, or he doesn't and is then set free from failing so he can succeed elsewhere. The manager wins regardless of the outcome. He either has the satisfaction of having helped turn around someone's performance (and possibly entire career) or the opportunity to replace someone who couldn't succeed, even when helped, with someone who can.

If the manager believes the underperforming salesperson is a "keeper" with true potential to succeed, then the goal of the informal remediation is to coach up the salesperson to an acceptable level of results. However, if the manager, for whatever reason, is convinced that the underachiever is not a "keeper" (attitude, work ethic, integrity issues, a misfit for the role, or just a complete mis-hire) I would suggest skipping informal remediation altogether. Save the grief, effort, time, and opportunity cost and move straight into a formal remediation to speed up the termination process.

There are various triggers indicating that it might be time to start a salesperson on an informal remediation plan. Every company, sales cycle, sales manager, and salesperson is unique, so it's almost impossible to make a blanket declaration about when to begin remediation. But having said that, here are some indicators that very well could mean it's time to begin an informal *coach-up or coach-out* process with one of your people:

▶ Results are not what they should be; the individual's performance lags behind that of the team.

▶ Something in your gut is telling you to put a giant question mark on this person. You're not exactly sure what is wrong, but you know something is not right.

▶ The salesperson does not seem to be *getting it* that you and the company are serious about results.

▶ You've had frustrating back-to-back 1:1 meetings with this person and she is not responding to your inquiries about her pipeline and activity in a way that reassures you that she is going to turn it around on her own.

► You become convinced that this salesperson needs not just a wakeup call but also clear marching orders and more intense direct supervision to have a better chance of succeeding.

► You truly believe that, for a period, overinvesting in this person (coaching and fieldwork) will pay significant long- and short-term dividends.

My coaching to sales leaders is simple: If you are not sure whether it's time to put someone on an informal remediation plan, then it's time. Do it.

Early is better than late. Nothing good comes from allowing underperformance, particularly mysterious underperformance, to go on longer than it should. Plus, as already mentioned, there is practically zero risk from beginning informal remediation with someone who is struggling. But there is much put at stake by waiting too long. Isn't it better to identify a problem when there is still time to fix it, or before it causes significant damage? When your car's engine doesn't sound right, is it wise to turn up the radio, ignore the indicator that something may be wrong, and hope the issue resolves itself? No, the smart move is to get that car in the shop and a qualified technician under the hood diagnosing the situation as quickly as possible. And that's exactly what you should be doing when there are warning lights on the dashboard for someone on your team.

Most managers wait too long to address underperformance. They suffer with poor results longer than they should. Nobody wins by ignoring potential failure. The culture suffers. The team's results suffer. And the team member who is not producing suffers while the situation typically worsens to the point that it's beyond repair. That is management malpractice, plain and simple.

Do not hesitate to begin an informal remediation. By its very nature, it is informal. You should not need to involve other executives or Human Resources. I am not saying you should actively avoid them; you just don't need to include them at this point. By all means, seek counsel from wise colleagues if you that feel would be beneficial. All I am suggesting is that you do your job by managing your team. If there's a sales team member requiring remediation, then start the process immediately.

This is made easier when you have already begun establishing a high-performance, results-focused culture (Chapter 18), and only seems natural when you are holding regular 1:1 results and pipeline-focused meetings (Chapter 20) with team members. Said differently, no one should be surprised that you, as the manager, are looking closely at results and are concerned by repeated underperformance.

Schedule a meeting or phone call with Johnny (the underperformer), and start it with something like this: "Johnny, it should not be a surprise that we are having this conversation today. I've discussed with you on numerous occasions that your results are not acceptable, and I am concerned that you are not turning it around as we both hoped you would. I want you to succeed. I believe you want to succeed. So we're meeting today because I want to help you get on the right track starting right now, because the status quo is unacceptable."

For some managers, that is an easy conversation. No sweat. In fact, they would consider what I am suggesting as rather wimpy compared to how they'd attack it. However, other conflict-avoiding managers are already getting sweaty palms and an upset stomach just imagining this hard conversation. Either way, it needs to happen. But it doesn't require raised voices, foul language, or angry threats. Alternatively, at this point, it also doesn't need a cheerleading, overly optimistic manager telling Johnny that he can do it, yes he can; if anyone can do it, Johnny can. Your job here is neither to threaten the salesperson nor to provide false hope. It's simply to share some hard truth that things need to change.

There are two critical characteristics of a successful remediation. First, there must be crystal clear expectations of what the manager is requiring the salesperson to achieve. It is not acceptable to tell the salesperson that he needs to "show improvement." Spell. It. Out. Specifically, what kind of improvement? "Johnny, I understand that you may not necessarily be able to close X number of new deals or Y dollars in the next sixty days. However, we need to put a firm stake in the ground to evaluate your progress. Here's what I am asking you to commit to as a demonstration that you are serious about turning around your performance (the following numbers are for illustration purposes only and have no meaning):

In the next sixty days, you need to have

1. Secured eighteen discovery meetings with named target accounts

2. Created eight new opportunities in the pipeline, two of which need to reach Phase M and two more need to get to Phase N.

"Johnny, are we clear on the expectations?" Johnny nods. You continue, "I'd like you to write up a mini-plan naming the specific existing accounts and prospects that you are going to pursue for those eighteen meetings. Within two days, I also want to see your planning calendar for the next two months so I can arrange to spend some time working with you in the field. And you and I will begin meeting every week instead of every month. When we meet each week, first you'll update me on your progress and then I'll be happy to spend the rest of the time helping and coaching you. All right, Johnny, repeat back what we just agreed on so I know we're on the same page."

The second critical characteristic for a successful remediation is that the salesperson fully grasps that he is 100 percent responsible for hitting the targets you establish with him. Salespeople are really good at making excuses and deflecting blame—particularly when put under the microscope. The manager's job is to ensure that the salesperson "owns" his future results and understands that you have no interest in hearing his rationale if he does not accomplish what was agreed to.

Last year I worked with a young national sales manager who had just taken over a team of veteran regional managers. This sales team had lived without serious accountability for decades. The new manager had his work cut out for him. One of the perennial underperformers managed an important territory on the West Coast. In every coaching conversation, I'd ask how it was going with Fred out west. The manager was becoming increasingly frustrated because Fred had an excuse for everything. I figured at some point that the manager would lose his cool and put Fred in his place, but it wasn't happening. Finally, he asked me how to handle Fred's continual excuses.

My response was swift and simple: "Tell Fred that he is the CEO of his territory. It's his job to produce results. Period. He manages the richest and most populous territory in the United States yet is regularly at the bottom of the sales rankings. Let him know that you are no longer interested in listening to his rationale for why he has not done. It's his job to place X amount of new and amount of business every month. Tell him that you how he is going to accomplish that next month, and if he is short again, there is going to be a problem. Offer to help him; offer to travel with him. But the second he starts to point the finger at anyone or anything else, stop him immediately! Remind him that it's his territory and he is responsible for what he does or doesn't produce."

In order to resolve performance issues, the salesperson must take full responsibility for results. The salesperson who refuses to sign on the bottom line and be fully accountable for what he produces is sending a very clear message that he's not interested in remediation. In those cases, the salesperson is asking you to replace him, and it's your job to oblige.

I spend very little time consulting about formal remediation. The reality is that once informal remediation and *coaching up* has failed to create the desired change, it's time to *coach out*. Quickly. While I encourage sales managers to put their heart and brainpower to work in efforts to save a "keeper" salesperson during an informal remediation, once that fails, it's time for the manager to pull back. I've yet to see an underperformer who didn't turn it around with help during informal remediation do so on his own during the formal stage. In other words, formal remediation is now a formality to remove that person from your team. You made your best reasonable effort to no avail. Get HR involved and follow your company's termination procedures with a clean conscience. Turn your attention to replacing that individual and coaching other team members. Your work with this person is done.

Recruiting Top Talent Requires Intentionality

I get a little nervous when executives brag that they have almost no turnover on their sales teams. While I appreciate their pride in a highly tenured sales force and satisfaction in the fact that people don't voluntarily leave their company, that isn't always indicative of a high-performance team. Often, it's the opposite. A sales team with zero turnover typically values longevity over results. Not that I'm advocating a Jack Welch approach of pruning the bottom 10 percent of employees each year, but it is hard to conceive that a high-performance culture wouldn't push laggards out the door—either by force or by choice.

It follows, then, that leaders who do not tolerate underperformance must excel at replacing those departing their teams. If you take seriously the responsibility of remediating or replacing underperformers, it is only logical that recruiting and placing new talent becomes an important part of the job.

Recruiting for the manager is much like prospecting for the salesperson. It's very important but typically not perceived as urgent. Recruiting, like prospecting, doesn't call you; you need to call it. We don't default to recruiting mode. There's always something easier, more attractive, or more urgent vying for our attention.

There are two critical keys to becoming a better recruiter. The first is to maintain a list of key referral sources and potential candidates. Just like a top sales hunter can always put her fingers on her target account list, the sales leader must be able to do the same. It would be too daunting to face starting from scratch every time you leapt into recruiting mode. Maintain a segmented list. In one section, list your best referral sources for new sales hires: customers, industry contacts, suppliers, your own salespeople, and other highly networked people in your sphere of influence. In the other segment, create a running list of actual candidates. Some managers refer to this as "building their bench." Managers who excel at recruiting monitor the depth and strength of people on their bench. They want to ensure that there is always a healthy pool of candidates available to them when the need arises. Think how different that approach is from that of the typical sales manager who ignores recruiting until he urgently needs to fill a hole.

The other key to becoming a successful recruiter is to carve out regular time on your calendar to focus exclusively on recruiting. As I just said, recruiting rarely calls you; you need to proactively pursue it. Similar to how we ask salespeople to dedicate specific time blocks for proactive prospecting, we must do the same for recruiting. The only way you'll dedicate time to recruiting is if you schedule appointments with yourself to actually do it! Open your calendar and plug in a few hours of recruiting time (or however long you deem appropriate for your situation) each month. That will ensure that you have "time" set aside to work both referral sources and candidates.

Many of you are likely wondering why I have not addressed three of the most popular vehicles for recruiting: job board services like CareerBuilder or Monster.com, LinkedIn, and search firms. My honest answer is that I stay away from consulting clients in these areas. Searching for candidates is a unique specialty and enormous industry. There are experts in all three of those search methods much more qualified than I. Each method has its own advantages and disadvantages, and a cursory review would not do the topic justice. This editorial comment I will make, however: In my experience, sales leaders who were really good at finding and attracting top talent were masters at working referral sources, and they dedicated significant chunks of time to recruiting.

While I do not help clients find candidates, I do love meeting with and interviewing prospective new hires. Everything around interviewing fascinates me—from the varying approaches taken by managers and companies conducting the interviews to the way candidates present themselves.

Aside from all the obvious qualities to evaluate during an interview—Is the candidate qualified, likable, trustworthy, professional, a good fit? Would I buy from this person? Will she raise the bar for my team?—I am looking to determine if this person can sell by observing how she handles herself and how she responds to two very specific questions.

First, I want to see if this salesperson makes the interview about herself or about the company. In general, I find that most interviewers talk too much and provide too much guidance to the interviewee. We are interviewing someone for a sales position, so let's see how she handles a sales situation. Is she comfortable? Does she have a plan? Is she prepared with great questions? Does she seek to truly understand what the company needs or why people succeed or fail in the role? Is she looking to determine if she is a good fit, or just interested in promoting herself?

Ask These Two Killer Questions During Every Interview

I save two sets of questions for the end of every interview. One takes us beyond theory and philosophy and provides a clear look at how the candidate has sold in the past. The other question offers a glimpse into how the candidate thinks and will approach the job.

Tell me about the last two significant deals you won due to your own proactive sales effort. Share the whole story from beginning to end. How did you identity or create the opportunity? How did you "get in"? Describe the discovery process. Tell me about the various stakeholders. How did you build interest and consensus? Take me through the chronology of the various conversations and meetings all the way through presenting, proposing, negotiating, and closing the deal.

A true sales winner loves this question because it provides an opportunity to strut her stuff. The poseur typically panics when asked for this level of detail. The first thing I am looking for is how difficult it is for the candidate to come up with recent success stories. That alone tells me a lot. From there, I'm trying to ascertain whether this is a true salesperson who understands how to create and advance opportunities, or if this candidate is just an order taker. How this question is answered either causes me to fall deeply in love with the candidate or has me throwing out a giant yellow caution flag. I'm looking for sales winners who have won in the past and know what to do and why they do it.

This final set of questions shows how the candidate views the role and will attack (or not attack) it: *Let's assume we hired you and you started on the first of the month. After getting you oriented to the company (for however long was appropriate), an email address, and business cards, we turned you loose. In fact, let's pretend that both your manager and I headed off to Hawaii for ninety days. Completely left on your own, I'd like you to sketch out how you'd approach the job. Where would you start? What would you do? Where would you go to learn more or for help when you needed it? If your manager sat you down on day ninety-one, what would you be able to tell him you accomplished in the market while he was away?*

After setting up that ninety-day scenario, I'm always curious to see candidates' reactions and how much clarification they request before answering. I instruct them to take as much time as needed to think it over before responding, and I encourage them to sketch out their thoughts on paper or the whiteboard. Some candidates craft pretty amazing plans, while others look at me in disbelief before they start shooting nonsense from the hip without giving it much thought. I promise that if you ask candidates both of these killer interview questions you will walk away with a much better feel for whether you want to add them to your team.

CHAPTER 24

Strategic Targeting: Point Your Team in the Right Direction

I have addressed leading the team, creating a healthy culture, and managing talent, so it's time to turn attention to the final critical piece of the sales management framework—ensuring that your team has a basic sales process in place.

Selecting Target Customers and Prospects Is Too Important to Take for Granted

I deploy the simplest of models to help sales teams gain clarity on executing a successful new business development–focused sales effort. The very first step in the model involves selecting what I call *targets*, which are simply the named existing customers and prospective customers that a salesperson identifies and commits to pursuing for new business.

This critical step is often overlooked by sales managers, who take for granted that their people have well-thought-out lists and are calling on the right targets. But selecting targets is too important to leave solely up to your salespeople. The harsh truth is that even the most talented people will fail if they're pursuing the wrong targets, which is something no manager can afford! As the leader, you want to have input into whom your team members are targeting. It is a rare opportunity to be strategic, to set direction. If you are ultimately responsible for leading your team into battle and assume ownership of the ensuing results, shouldn't you be heavily involved in directing the attack?

As hard as this is to grasp, the truth is that many salespeople and sales teams operate day after day without a list of strategic targets. Why? Because they live in reactive mode, responding only to leads or to customers that raise their hands. But the moment we ask them to shift into proactive mode, the natural and necessary first question is "Who should we target?" Since a salesperson's target list effectively drives how that individual spends proactive selling time, I believe that management should be very much involved in determining which accounts make the list, who should be targeted.

Stop the Milk Run and Turn off the Sales Autopilot

When asked to describe the characteristics of a good target list, the first word out of my mouth is *strategic*. Then I joke that *strategic* is just a fancy word that means we actually put some thought into which customers and prospects end up on a salesperson's list. So many salespeople seem to turn off their brains when it comes to targeting. In companies that deploy territory managers, I see these salespeople running the *same routes* they were assigned five years ago, when first taking the position. If it's the second Tuesday of the month, they must be in Abilene, because that's where the person who had the job before them was each second Tuesday! The fact that there are no important accounts left in Abilene is an afterthought.

Territory manager salespeople are famous for brainlessly doing what many call "the milk run." Long ago they stopped thinking strategically. They have forgotten that the goal is to grow the business, not to play caretaker for a piece of geography. Read that last sentence once more. We've got a decent percentage of salespeople who see their primary job as managing the territory (a piece of earth) instead of maximizing revenue. Whose fault is that? It's the sales manager's fault for not emphasizing a strategic approach to targeting.

I challenge sales managers to invest more energy helping territory salespeople and account managers evaluate their lists and segment accounts into logical categories. Force sales team members to step back and see the big picture. Stop talking about *account coverage* and start talking about growth opportunities. I regularly admonish salespeople that if an existing customer is not large, growable, or at risk, then that account is not worthy of their time.

Territory managers and outside salespeople are not alone when it comes to disengaging their minds. Plenty of inside sales teams and sales hunters operate mindlessly, too. It's not a "milk run" per se, because this behavior occurs in the office. These sellers operate on autopilot. They start their day by clicking on the CRM activity screen and up pop thirty sales tasks to be completed. One by one, day after day, they click through their task list. Sure, at one point, those scheduled tasks were meaningful, but over time, salespeople drift into autopilot mode. They stop looking at the big picture or thinking about what they are doing. The sales airplane simply flies itself on a predetermined course based on information and scheduled tasks entered long ago.

Is there anything wrong with diligently executing scheduled sales tasks? No, of course not. We want our salespeople to stay on top of leads and opportunities. But when the behavior becomes rote and devoid of further thinking about whom a salesperson *should* be targeting for business, it is time to get concerned. I'll ask a salesperson which prospects he is proactively pursuing right now/this week/this month, and many, without even pausing, will say, "whichever accounts pop up on my screen." Or, I'll be visiting a client and stop at an underperformer's desk to see if/how he's implementing the coaching he received. When I inquire as to how he is doing and what he's working on, typically I get a loud, tired sigh as he points to a list of tasks in his CRM that has turned red. He'll tell me that he's really behind and needs to get caught up—of course, with no thought as to whether "catching up" on overdue sales tasks will produce any meaningful opportunities in the pipeline.

Managers should call regular *targeting time-outs* to help their sales team stop doing milk runs or flying on autopilot. Remind yourself and your team members that the big goal is always to grow revenue, and the most effective way to accomplish that is to ensure that you're pursuing the right targets. Yes, a high-frequency sales attack is preferable to a low-frequency effort, but that principle applies only when the sales force is attacking the best targets for new business. Call time-out. Have your salespeople push pause to ask themselves:

► Do the target accounts I've been pursuing provide the best chance of winning new business?

► Have I fallen into a rut because I'm comfortable calling the same customers and prospects over and over?

► Is it time to reevaluate how I segment my existing accounts (or manage my territory) so my best effort goes toward the most strategic opportunities?

► How can I clean up my open tasks in the CRM so I know I'm working leads and opportunities most likely to produce results?

It bears repeating: There are no awards for doing the most work, making the most calls, or driving the most miles. Sales activity is good activity only if it's focused on the right target customers.

When It Comes to Targeting, Less Is Often More

Salespeople typically prefer longer target lists and larger territories. Having more named prospects and customers gives salespeople comfort. They not only feel more important when charged with what feels like more responsibility, they also feel protected. The common wisdom is that the more accounts on your list, the better chance that one will raise its hand and present a new opportunity. Many salespeople react negatively when asked to narrow their focus or give up certain accounts. They fear "missing out" should an opportunity emerge from some dark corner of their territory or from a prospect they've yet to meet. Much like a toddler, salespeople like to put their arms around their giant territories (lists) and scream "Mine!" when in danger of losing any target accounts.

Similarly, sales managers and company executives gain a (false) sense of comfort when they think the sales team is attacking a large swath of potential customers. They (mistakenly) believe that more is better: The bigger the list, the busier the salespeople will stay, and the greater the chance of growing the business.

As you've surmised by now, I maintain a contrarian view on this topic. When it comes to targeting, and even more so when specifically hunting for new business, less is often more. Shorter, finite, workable target lists provide the proactive salesperson the best chance of creating new opportunities and winning new business. When the target list is too long, salespeople have difficulty focusing their attack. Overwhelmed by the volume of targets, they often end up shooting randomly in various directions. This scattershot approach prevents a sales attack from gaining traction. Particularly when prospecting, it can take multiple touches (attempts) to grab a prospect's attention. Unfocused salespeople, distracted by the sheer volume of targets on their lists, rarely take repeated shots at the same target. Instead, they deploy a "one and done" strategy. They'll take one shot at one account and move on to the next. This shoot and run cycle continues. Shoot and run, shoot and run, shoot and run. Unless they're incredibly lucky with these random one-shot attempts, this feeble type of prospecting usually fails to uncover opportunities.

However, when a salesperson, with management's input, commits to a focused sales attack against a strategically selected, finite, workable list of targets, good things happen! Less produces more. A wider spray shotgun approach may work well for marketing, but the sniper rifle is the preferred sales tool. Across a variety of industries and sales roles, I regularly see salespeople become more effective and create more new opportunities when they narrow their focus. The reality is that you can only proactively pursue a finite number of targets. That number will vary depending on the complexity of the sale, length of the sales cycle, and how difficult it is to earn a target customer's time and attention. So, while I can't offer a generic number that is right for your specific situation, the two words that I find most helpful are *finite* and *workable*. We want each salesperson to have enough targets to *work*, but not too many that she can't take repeated shots at the same targets over a dedicated period of time. Very often it takes multiple attempts on the same target for the salesperson to earn her way in and begin the sales process.

Instead of taking for granted that your team members are aiming at the right targets, take advantage of this important opportunity to point them in the right direction.

CHAPTER 25

The Sales Manager Must Ensure That the Team Is Armed for Battle

Once targets are selected, the manager has two primary responsibilities. The first is to ensure that the troops are armed with the necessary sales weapons to head into battle. And, second, the manager must make sure that team members become proficient at firing these weapons.

Similar to how sales managers often take for granted that their people are focused on the right targets, it's not uncommon for managers to simply assume that team members are properly equipped for battle. Assuming is dangerous, and sending your troops on the attack without the proper weapons or training for how to use them is even worse! Sales leaders, please hear me: If you want to hold your teams accountable for producing results, then you must be fully accountable for equipping them to win.

The Sales Manager Does Not Need to Be the Sales Expert

Before diving further into this topic, let me make an important point that will give some of you comfort. I don't believe that you need to be a sales expert to effectively lead a sales team to victory. You've already read about the power of a healthy, results-focused culture where the manager regularly meets 1:1 with each salesperson, conducts productive sales team meetings, works in the field alongside team members, and becomes a master at managing talent (the Four Rs). All of those aspects of sales management can be beautifully handled by someone who is not a sales expert. While, in this chapter, I am absolutely making the case that you are 100 percent responsible for your team being properly equipped to sell, that does not necessarily translate into you having to be the local expert, sales coach, and trainer. You need not be the sales technician who builds the weapons and then trains your people how to fire them.

I've observed many situations where very effective sales leaders possessed little sales acumen or experience. This is most common in smaller organizations where an owner or senior executive also serves as part-time sales manager. And while it's less common in larger companies with professionally run sales teams, I've met quite a few people who ended up in big company sales management roles without having been a salesperson first. These executives had no problem admitting that they were not sales experts and were glad to seek the help of others when it came to equipping and training their sales teams.

The larger point I want to convey here is that while you need not be the expert, that is not a pass to look the other way when it comes to arming the team. The sales team requires a full arsenal of essential weapons and help to become proficient at using them, whether it comes from you, an associate within your organization, or an outside expert. You are responsible for making that happen.

There Is No More Critical Weapon than the "Sales Story"

There are a few dozen weapons in the salesperson's arsenal, ranging from email, LinkedIn, and voicemail, to probing questions, presentations, facility tours, and references. None, however, is more important than what I call the "sales story." What some call a value proposition and others refer to as an elevator pitch, I call the story. Basically, it's a collection of compelling talking points that when used properly becomes the single most valuable sales weapon. Part of the reason the story is so critical is that bits and pieces of it end up in every other weapon. Talking points from the story make their way into LinkedIn profiles, proactive telephone call outlines, voicemails, face-to-face sales calls, demos, webinars, presentations, and proposals. If it involves any aspect of selling, there's a really good chance that the sales story makes an appearance.

The most popular chapter in my first book is titled "Sharpening Your Sales Story." It seems that just about every company, sales team, and salesperson admits that their story has room for improvement. What astonishes me (and keeps me employed) is that when I go into a company and ask a handful of executives and salespeople to "Tell me about [your company name]," I get as many versions of the story as the number of people I ask! Even worse than the wide variety is that so little of what I hear is compelling.

There are three common sins salespeople commit when sharing their story. The first sin is that most stories are too complex. They take too long to tell and are not easy to follow. That's a problem indeed. It shouldn't take ten minutes or ten PowerPoint slides to get someone's attention, share how you help your clients, and succinctly explain your offering.

The second and third common story sins go hand-in-hand. Salespeople are often boring and self-focused. They begin by talking about their company and their offerings. What could be less appealing to a potential customer than the salesperson leading with what his company does and how long it has been in business? You chuckle reading it, but that is exactly how most salespeople start their sales story. "We do this, that, and the other thing. We've been in business thirty-nine years. We are privately held. Here are pictures of our facilities." I may injure the next salesperson who puts a picture of his company's buildings in a presentation!

If one of your primary jobs as the sales leader is to arm the team with effective sales weapons, then sales process priority number one has to be sharpening the team's most critical weapon. A succinct, compelling, customer-issue-focused, differentiating story changes everything. An effective story:

- ► Gives salespeople confidence to prospect

- ► Changes the dynamic of the sales dance and positions your salespeople as experts and consultants

- ► Gets the customer or prospect's attention

- ► Helps customers to see clearly and quickly that what you sell addresses the very issues they face

- ► Enables the salesperson to better articulate the true value your solution delivers

- ► Warms up the customer to respond to probing questions

- ► Justifies your premium price and position in the market

- ► Differentiates your company from competitors

- ► Makes salespeople even more proud of their company

If that list of benefits doesn't compel you to put forth a supreme effort to sharpen your sales story, nothing will. It's hard to think of a better gift to your salespeople (and company) than equipping them with a killer story and helping them put it to use in all of their other weapons.

Stop Hoping for the Magic Sales Bullet and Focus on the Basics

It's amusing how much energy is spent searching for the magic sales bullet. Executives and salespeople alike seem to live in the perpetual hope that they'll discover the new secret that guarantees unlimited qualified leads, a full pipeline, and the ability to close every deal at full price. Well, I've got bad news, good news, and a rather transparent confession to share.

The bad news is that there is no magic bullet or secret sauce. Despite all the hype about the latest and greatest new sales approaches, processes, techniques, tools, and toys that you *must have* to win at sales today, there's no one thing or new thing that will alter your team's performance or the course of history. I'm sorry to break it to you, but there is no sales leadership shortcut that will magically change everything, and the people peddling that nonsense are nothing more than liars and charlatans looking to capitalize on your desire for a quick fix.

There is also some very good news. The basics of selling still work! The overwhelming majority of widely accepted sales truths are still true today. Contrary to what we read and hear from the nouveau experts, sales leaders who focus on the tried and true fundamentals of selling, and have their salespeople do the same, experience significant success.

My transparent confession? After almost every consulting or speaking engagement, I receive consistent feedback. Whether it's from a senior vice president of global business development for a multi-billion-dollar company, the president of a $200 million firm, or the managing partner of a $10 million tech start-up, I hear the same thing over and over: "Thank you for setting us straight and providing a fresh perspective on the basics of sales (or sales leadership). We have either forgotten or moved away from these things that we know work. *Nothing* you shared with us was radically new or too complex and confusing to implement."

I love hearing that! I'm not ashamed that I haven't invented some silly newfangled tool promising to make you a quick buck or fix *every-thing* that's wrong with your sales team. The harsh truth is that those in sales and sales leadership who understand and master the basics thrive, and those who ignore them perpetually struggle.

My hope is that sharing the bad news, good news, and that confession motivates you to take a hard look at not just the sales management basics presented in Part Two of this book. I hope that you'll also reevaluate the strength of your sales team's most fundamental weapons as well. Along with the sales story, there are a handful of others deployed by your people on a daily basis. How much more effective could your team be if they became highly proficient at firing these weapons?

For example, when was the last time you did a thorough review of how your sales team members prepare for, structure, and conduct initial/discovery sales calls? Do you even have some type of "standard" sales call structure in place or minimum expectations for what should take place before, during, and after a sales call? If you don't, you should. That initial sales call with a prospective customer can set the tone for the whole relationship. We work so darn hard to get in front of the right people at the right company. Wouldn't it make sense to put our best foot forward when we finally get there? And wouldn't you feel better as the leader knowing that your people were all operating under a set of standard expectations for how sales calls should flow?

This book isn't the venue to include a treatise on how to structure and conduct winning consultative sales calls. That topic alone could be its own book, and I devoted two full chapters to it in *New Sales. Simplified*. But let me offer some helpful questions to encourage sales leaders to start tackling the topic:

- ► What is the minimum acceptable amount of research and information gathering that must be done during pre-call planning?

- ► Does your company have some type of prescribed structure for sales calls that outlines the various stages from beginning to end?

- ► What materials and tools should salespeople have with them

195

on sales calls? And which tools are better left at home or saved for later in the sales process? (Hint: a projector.)

► Have you worked through the best way to set up the sales call by sharing the agenda and seeking the customer's input and buy-in?

► How well do your people share a succinct version of the sales story to position themselves as customer-issue-focused expert problem solvers before launching into probing questions?

► Are team members armed with insightful probing questions that not only help them learn more about the customer's situation, but also demonstrate your company's familiarity with the kinds of issues likely on the mind of the customer?

► Is every person on your sales team clear that discovery must precede presentation, and do they know how to respond when a customer insists that they start with a capabilities overview?

► How comfortable are salespeople at fleshing out potential objections or securing a customer's commitment to next steps?

► What processes are in place following a sales call? What information gets shared or recorded and what happens with that information?

Obviously, those questions just scratch the surface of what takes place during sales calls, but it is a safe bet that a good portion of the sales management population would not be confident or comfortable with their answers. Honestly, that's the point I'm trying to make. Too many managers are caught up in their underwear sitting in corporate meetings and doing all kinds of non-sales-leadership activities. Or, they're buried in statistical minutiae spewing from their CRM. Or worse, they're out shopping for some new sales enablement tool that promises to turn underperformers into quota-crushers. All the while they're playing good corporate citizen, CRM jockey, or sales tool super-shopper, their sales team is out making pathetic sales call after pathetic sales call.

Do you see the madness? I honestly don't know how we got here, but this nonsense has to stop. Sales leaders need to lead their sales teams. Leading translates to pointing their team in the right direction, preparing them for battle, and arming them with the basic weapons they need to win. If you are too overwhelmed to ensure that your sales force can tell a compelling story, conduct a proper sales call, deliver a powerful presentation, or craft a winning proposal, then something is fundamentally broken at your company. You may have the most energizing executive committee meetings and the coolest graphics on your CRM dashboard, but if your sales team can't execute the basics well, you're not doing your job and sales results will suffer.

CHAPTER 26

Sales Managers Must Monitor the Battle and Be Ruthless with Their Time

The first two steps in our simple sales process model, strategic targeting and arming the team, are preparatory in nature. Both are foundational to launching an effective sales attack. This third step, monitoring the battle, is an ongoing process. Any good commander keeps abreast of how the troops are performing and intercedes as necessary. The same is true for sales leaders who monitor the sales battle through personal observation, sales reports, pipeline reports, 1:1 and team meetings, and individual business plans.

Individual Business Plans Are a Gift to the Sales Leader

One of the most powerful sales management tools is an annual business plan prepared by each member of your sales team. Yet, few companies have salespeople write and present individual plans. And of the few that do, even fewer use those plans as a living, breathing management tool throughout the course of the year.

I am a huge proponent of creating a basic template and assigning each member of the sales team to draft and present an annual plan. Too much good comes from this exercise not to do it, and even beyond the initial benefits, these plans end up being an incredible long-term gift to the sales manager.

We've all heard of studies concluding that people who put their goals in writing are more successful. But getting specific sales goals on paper is just the tip of the business plan iceberg. Drafting plans forces salespeople to step back from the daily grind to think about the big picture. It also helps reinforce the point that it's *their* territory or book of business, and they must take ownership of the strategies they will employ and the results they'll produce. This exercise also causes sales-people to reflect back on the previous year to determine what worked and what didn't. It's so basic, yet I often hear profound answers when sales reps are asked what worked in the past year that they need to do more of, or what strategies or techniques flubbed and should be abandoned. We like to joke about the definition of insanity (doing the same thing over and over and expecting a different result), but it's no laughing matter. How many struggling salespeople continue down the same path hoping things will change? Too many.

There is no one-size-fits-all business plan template. Each manager has the freedom to tailor his team's plan to his own preferences and what makes best sense for that particular business. Let me offer a simple template for an individual salesperson's plan that has proved helpful as a starting point:

- ► *Goals—What are you going to achieve?* We always start with the end in mind. Possible categories in this section would include total revenue or gross margin goals for the year, number of new accounts or new pieces of business acquired, dollars sold to both existing and new accounts, and specific product-mix goals. You might even ask the rep to "name and claim" the monster account or dream client he or she will nail this year. As an aside, it is amazing how many salespeople actually close a deal with a dream client in the year they named it in their plan.

▶ *Strategies—How are you going to do it?* Where is it going to come from? In this section, I like to ask questions about market focus, target account lists, major cross-sell opportunities, most growable, and most at-risk accounts. I want the salespeople to articulate what new approaches will get them in front of prospects, and how they will better penetrate current customers. If it's a territory management job, I ask the salespeople to revisit their yearly planning calendar and discuss how they can be more intentional in segmenting accounts and covering the territory.

▶ *Actions—What are you going to do?* In this section, we want to hear about activity and metrics. What's "The Math"? How many calls, initial face-to-face meetings, presentations, etc. will the salesperson commit to making? How will the salesperson block calendar time to prospect and pursue pure new business? To what key activity goals will he or she be accountable?

▶ *Obstacles—What's in the way?* I don't believe in excuses and, as the sales manager, neither should you! I firmly believe that almost every salesperson could tell you on day one what is likely to get in the way of achieving goals for the year. So ask for a list of known obstacles right up front, in the business plan. This allows management to address and help remove these obstacles, or call them what they are—lame excuses. Failure is not an option. The last thing you want is to discover an issue nine months into the year that the salesperson was concerned about on day one. Obstacles take many forms: lack of training or knowledge, prohibitive policies, travel budgets, old technology, the anti-sales department, family issues, etc.

Just ask. Believe me, your people will have no trouble making a list.

► *Personal Development, Growth, and Motivation—How do you want to grow this year and what will keep you motivated?* If we are not growing, then we are dying. Salespeople need to take responsibility for their own personal development. Ask them how they intend to do that. Are there courses or conferences they would like to attend? Will they seek a mentor or outside coaching, or possibly commit to reading certain sales books or blogs? Are there areas where they need to develop professionally? It's also beneficial to have salespeople share some of their personal philosophies about sales and what they will do to keep themselves motivated throughout the year. You will get some really fun answers and learn a lot about what drives your people.

Simply having your team write plans is powerful in and of itself. However, there are even greater benefits when salespeople present their plans in front of the sales team and management. Team members learn from each other as strategies are shared. Smart strategies are applauded while foolish ones are challenged. The very act of publicly declaring a plan creates a feeling of instant accountability. Many benefits accrue to the sales manager from these presentations. You get a great read on who *gets it* and who doesn't. Which of your people invested the effort to draft a thoughtful plan, and which waited to the last minute and threw something together the night before the meeting? Even better, you have the opportunity to see who presents well and who is awful in front of the room. It should concern you when one of your people bombs in front of his peers. If that is how he comes across in his own conference room, how bad might he be when presenting to a customer?

My favorite aspect of the individual business plan is that it is a gift to the sales manager that keeps on giving all year. Before heading out to work with one of your people or when you're concerned someone on your team is off track, grab the person's business plan. Take a quick glance at the first few sections and make mental note of a few strategies he proposed and actions to which he committed. When you sit down with him ask some very simple leading questions. The conversation might go something like this:

"Hey, Doug, you seem a little unfocused. Let me ask you, in your business plan you committed to two strong strategies everyone really liked. The first was inviting prospects to one 'lunch and learn' event per month, and the other was intentionally pursuing three meetings with existing customers that have significant cross-sell upside. How are those strategies working for you? I haven't heard much about these cross-sell meetings and I don't remember seeing an expense report with food for even one 'lunch and learn.'"

Doug stumbles a bit and then tells you he hasn't gotten around to inviting prospects to a "lunch and learn" because he has so much else on his plate. You stop him dead in his tracks.

"Hold on, Doug. This was *your* business plan. You wrote it. You were the one who declared you would execute these strategies in order to achieve your sales goal, not me. So if this is no longer your plan, what are you going to do to make your numbers? And if this is your plan, it's time to start executing it!"

Take advantage of the fact that you have these plans from each of your people. They wrote them; they need to execute against them. Use these plans to regularly check up to see if team members are doing what they declared was necessary to succeed. What makes it so powerful is that you are able to use their own words to monitor their progress and hold them accountable. As I said, written individual business plans are a gift to the sales manager!

Insist on Getting the Reports You Need to Lead Your Team

Sales managers require accurate, timely, usable reports to monitor sales results and the pipeline. Do not compromise on this. There is zero excuse for your company not being able to furnish you with just about any report you desire. There is more computing power in the phones in our pockets than there was on the Apollo spacecraft that went to the moon. If you need a report, someone can create it! Oh, you'll get excuses from accounting people or the IT folks. They'll tell you that they don't have the data in a usable format, or that the company ERP system (like Oracle or SAP) makes it challenging to get a report the way you want it. Some joker will tell you, "We didn't purchase that module of the CRM system so we'll have to do a workaround if you really must have it that way." Sales manager, please hear me on this: Insist on getting the exact reports you need in the exact format you want them. It's okay if it takes some programmer a day to figure it out or an accountant has to crunch numbers into a spreadsheet and manually import some data. Be unreasonable. Do not compromise. Let them struggle with the workaround. Why am I so direct with this advice? Two easy reasons: First, if you truly believe that you need a particular report to monitor the sales attack, make good decisions, and help drive the business, then you should have it. Believe me, if you were the CEO and asked for a report that required lots of effort to create, you'd get it no questions asked.

The second reason you should insist on getting what you need is because these very same people whining that you're creating work for them will be the first ones pointing the finger at you when your sales team doesn't deliver as promised. These same accountants who don't want to be hassled with your report requests will be amazingly quick to generate their own reports showing that your sales team is discounting too frequently, spending too much, or falling short of sales and gross margin projections. I've seen this exact scenario play out and it's infuriating. Yes, I'm being extreme, and, no, I don't have a personal vendetta against accountants. I've just been around too many anti-sales organizations where the sales team, starting with the manager, doesn't get the respect it deserves. Figure out exactly how you would like to see sales results every month, by territory or salesperson or product line or customer or supplier, versus goal and versus last year, or any combination thereof that makes good sense to you. Then take your accounting or IT colleagues out to a nice lunch and tell them what you need. You pay for lunch and say please and thank you when making your request. And do not take "no" for an answer.

Successful Sales Managers Are Selfishly Productive

As we wind down our journey together through *Sales Management. Simplified.*, I'd like to circle back to my father's powerful words of wisdom from Chapter 1. The sales management role can be one of the most challenging jobs on the planet. Everyone wants a piece of you. Bosses, colleagues in other departments, and sales team members don't think twice about asking for your time or putting work on your plate. If you allow these people who don't really understand your job to dictate how you spend your time, you'll not only be more overwhelmed and more miserable, but you will fail at your most important job—leading the sales team to victory.

Working a bazillion hours and jamming your calendar with an obscene number of meetings doesn't make you more valuable. Or more productive. Living in a perpetually overwhelmed state should not be worn like a badge of honor. When caught in the daily grind, it's easy to forget this guiding principle: You were not hired to do work; you were put in your position to produce results. Let me say that again: Your *job* is to drive results. There is no prize for handling a bigger load, reading and sending hundreds of emails, attending endless meetings, or even planning monthly birthday parties. Being busy, even extremely busy, as such, can be worthless. That is particularly true when we're busy because we're playing good corporate citizen, putting on the fire chief's helmet, and burying ourselves in non-sales-leadership activities!

Today's reality is that everyone is busy. We're all over-connected, over-meeting-ed, over-emailed. So allowing yourself to live even more out of control and more out of breath doesn't make you better and more valuable, or even provide you with more job security. In fact, it may do the opposite.

The most successful, productive, effective executives exhibit a characteristic that I've termed *selfishly productive*. They are incredibly selfish but in an incredibly good way. These highly effective leaders are ruthless with their time. They jealously guard their calendars and protect their time as if it's their oxygen supply. They become absolute masters at saying that simple two-letter word: *No*.

Selfishly productive people outperform others for one simple reason: They maximize their time on high-value, high-payoff activities. These highly effective leaders time-block their calendars, filling up their days with undertakings they feel are most important. Time-blocking serves both a defensive and offensive purpose. From a defensive posture, filling your calendar with what you know you should be working on prevents that space from being available to others. It's freeing and energizing when someone invites you to a nonessential meeting to look in your calendar and see the time *already* reserved by you. "Sorry, I'm booked that afternoon with a high-priority project."

As an offensive weapon, time-blocking ensures that you have sufficient time carved out to invest in those high-value activities you've identified. You feel empowered when you take back control of your calendar. There is this wonderful feeling that comes from deciding for yourself how you will spend your time.

I don't live in a fantasy world or alternative universe. I am fully aware that there are demands on your time over which you have no control. There are mandatory meetings, people who need you, deals requiring approval, legitimate emergencies that disrupt your day. I get it. But what I also recognize (and observe in way too many companies) is that sales managers could work sixty-plus hours per week but never once get to their own priorities, and barely sniff work that might actually move the revenue needle. Isn't it fair to conclude that something is fundamentally broken when a drowning sales manager whose team isn't hitting its numbers is too busy to work in the field with his people or conduct a regular monthly 1:1 meeting with each salesperson?

Here's my challenge: How can you become more selfishly productive? What would it take to radically revamp your calendar so you were more in control? What might happen to your effectiveness as a sales leader and the performance of your sales team if you spent the vast majority of time focused on the high-value, high-payoff sales management priorities presented in Part Two of this book?

I wish you huge success in your current or future sales leadership role and offer my sincere thanks and appreciation for reading this book. If you'd like to keep up with me, I blog about sales, sales leadership, and productivity at www.newsalescoach.com, and my twitter handle is @mike_weinberg.

INDEX